MAKING WAR
in the
NAME OF GOD

MAKING WAR
in the
NAME OF GOD

CHRISTOPHER CATHERWOOD

CITADEL PRESS
Kensington Publishing Corp.
www.kensingtonbooks.com

CITADEL PRESS BOOKS are published by

Kensington Publishing Corp.
850 Third Avenue
New York, NY 10022

All Kensington titles, imprints, and distributed lines are available at special quantity discounts for bulk purchases for sales promotions, premiums, fund-raising, educational, or institutional use. Special book excerpts or customized printings can also be created to fit specific needs. For details, write or phone the office of the Kensington special sales manager: Kensington Publishing Corp., 850 Third Avenue, New York, NY 10022, attn: Special Sales Department; phone 1-800-221-2647.

First printing: September 2007

10 9 8 7 6 5 4 3 2 1

Printed in the United States of America

Library of Congress Control Number: 2007928675

ISBN-13: 978-0-8065-2785-7
ISBN-10: 0-8065-2785-4

To Gene Brissie,
Publisher, Literary Agent, and Editor,
Who gave me my big break
and to whom so many authors owe so much

and

To my wonderful wife, Paulette,
My Inspiration for All My Books,
Whose love and support makes them all possible

Contents

Acknowledgments

This book began life as a telephone conversation between two great men of the New York literary scene: Gene Brissie and Ed Claflin. Gene has moved responsibilities since then, but without the two of them this book would never have happened. It is their idea and I am deeply grateful to them both.

My wife, Paulette, is my constant inspiration, muse, help, best friend, companion, and many more things besides. (Even better, what I have written is only the half of it—it is no exaggeration.) So to her I give my warmest possible thanks, love, praise, and gratitude.

I am also very fortunate in having the splendid Gary Goldstein of Citadel Press as my editor, in place of Gene Brissie. I am most grateful for Gary's encouragement and for his forbearance when my teaching commitments and my gaining a doctorate meant that this manuscript arrived later than he had intended.

I began the writing of this in the splendid surroundings of the History Department of the University of Richmond, in Richmond, Virginia. This is the latest of many years in which they have appointed me their annual summer Writer in Residence, and I am honored to have this post yet once again, to write and finish my books. Professor Hugh West, the department chairman, made the Douglas Freeman Office mine again, and it is a great haven in which to work.

This year special thanks go to Professor John Gordon, the former History Department chairman, and his wife, Susan, who have been the embodiment of scholarly kindness, help, and assistance well beyond the call of duty. I am also very grateful to the legendary Professor John Treadway, for making his apartment free for me and for my wife to live in for another summer, and, this year, for installing a special desk there for me to use. Kathy Fuggett remains the department administrator without whom no academics could function; and this year the department gave me some great new bookshelves to store all the many books on the Crusades, the French Wars of Religion, and on the numerous other subjects I need to write this book.

The humanities librarian at the Boatwright Library, Jim Gwin, was as efficient, kind and helpful as ever, in spite of a major reconstruction of the library building this year, the history and religion sections included.

I was able to teach a course again this summer at the School of Continuing Education's annual summer school. Warmest possible thanks go to Dr. David Kitchen, who provided me with such a great number of students, and to Jane Dowrick, of the linked Osher Institute, for enabling me to teach retired people here in Richmond. The staff of the SCS, Professors Jim Narduzzi and Pat Brown, Cheryl Genovese and Ginnie Carlson, all deserve special thanks for another great year.

Ellis Billups Jr. and Marge Musial proved invaluable in technical assistance to a technically challenged historian. Fred Anderson, of the VBHS, has also been as encouraging a support as ever.

Finally at Richmond, the wonderful bookstore deserves a special mention, since, as every year, they have been kindness and assistance personified. Roger Brooks, Victoria Halman, Douglass Young, Sharon Crumley, Lydia Gale, and all other members of the staff there were as excellent this year as they have been for many years past. Few universities can be as fortunate as Richmond in the uniquely high quality of the service provided, and I, for one, am especially grateful to all of them once more.

I am also fortunate in my links in Cambridge, England. St Edmund's College Cambridge is an exceptionally relaxed and friendly place, and my thanks go here to too many people to mention, but with special gratitude to all the Senior Combination Room regulars, to the master for formalizing my rights, to Moira Gardner for making that effective, and to the astronomer Simon Mitton and all my fellow coffee drinkers for making the college such an enjoyable place to be.

Warm thanks go as always to Dr. Philip Towle, the emeritus director of the Centre of International Studies, to Dr. Eugenio Biagini of the history faculty, and to Professor Chris Andrew for his seminar. I have the great pleasure of teaching bright American student exchange students from Tulane, Wake Forest, Rice, Villanova and other U.S. universities through the IN-STEP Program; and its director and administrator, Professor Geoffrey Williams and his wife, Janice, deserve especial praise for their consistent support, kindness, and encouragement over many happy years of teaching.

This year I received a PhD by publication through the University of East Anglia, based in Norwich, England. Not only is UEA one of Britain's top twenty universities, but its History Department is one of only a tiny handful to get a 5** rating — a much higher ranking than that of many far more internationally famous institutions. Warmest possible thanks and gratitude therefore go to my supervisor, the legendary John Charmley, who has been all one could ever hope for in such a task, and much more besides, and to his assistant Judy Sparks, who made it all administratively possible.

Some of this book was also written in the beautiful home outside of Atlanta, Georgia, of two dear friends, Don and Emilie Wade. I thank them both for their years of kindness and hospitality, and for all they have meant to me and to my wife over so long a time. Another part was written at the new home in Virginia of my brother-in-law Sterling Moore, and his wife, Janet. I am blessed in so many of my in-laws, and a special thanks goes to one who is no longer with us as I write this.

My late father-in-law, John S. Moore, the distinguished church historian, died while I was beginning the study for this work. His kindness and careful scholarship have been inspirations. He will be most sorely missed—it is hard to envisage a book of mine appearing without his sage insights and thoughtful comments.

Finally, I learned my love of history through my parents, Frederick and Elizabeth Catherwood, and many of my other books have been written in the atmospheric fifteenth-century upper floor of their house in Cambridgeshire. My gratitude to them and to John Moore is profound and lifelong.

Cambridge, England, and Richmond, Virginia

❖ 1 ❖

RELIGIOUS WAR
A Brief Introduction

Slay the unbelievers where you find them . . .
> —Quran, Sura 9:5 the "Sword verse"

The atrocity of September 11 is a violation of Islamic law and ethics.
> —The late Sheikh Zaki Badawi, of the
> Muslim College in London, after 9/11

CONFUSED?

This book will look at the long history of religious warfare in all its aspects, part of what my editor at Citadel Press has rightly described as the "dark heart of man." It is a phenomenon that one might legitimately call humanity's dirty secret, especially since religion is also regarded, a few hard-line atheists apart, as primarily a tool for peace and harmony, rather than for war.

I will not be considering only war between Muslims and Christians, since religious warfare is far wider in scope than that. For example, we will see that, as well as going to war against each other, Muslims and Christians have fought within their respective faith, such as during the intra-Islamic warfare of the seventh century, and the 150 years or so of European history usually named the Wars of Religion, when Catholics fought

1

Protestants. In some parts of the world today, Muslims and Christians are the victims, not the perpetrators of aggression, notably in India, where the same extremist Hindu organization that murdered Mahatma Gandhi is still encouraging the massacre of Indians not of the majority faith.

In other words, where you find people, you find war, and since most people alive today are religious in some form or another, religion is often the excuse made to slaughter others on a grand scale.

However, those faiths around today—what British expert Anthony Smith calls "salvation religions"—usually teach that violence is normally wrong, except in specially permitted circumstances. I cannot simply go up to someone I dislike and beat him over the head, however much I might want to do so, because by the standards of most faiths today that would be morally wrong. What applies to an individual is also true of a much larger group of people, such as a nation state or a religious community.

Yet, since the dawn of time, individuals have been killing one another and nations have warred against each other—in our own era, with devastating effects, since the tools modernity uses for slaughter are far more efficient than were the simple weapons of days gone by.

In more recent times, warfare has been for reasons other than religion: for national gain, for economic resources, for ideological conquest. Hitler did not wipe out 6 million Jews and over 20 million Russians for religious reasons, but for a warped belief in the racial superiority of the German people. Communism is profoundly antireligious, and it was responsible for the deaths of tens of millions more during the last century.

Yet the excuse made by so many over millennia to murder in the name of religion has not gone away, be it the slaughter of over 8,000 Muslim men at Srebrenica in 1995 to the better-known carnage in Washington, DC, and New York of September 11, 2001, when over 3,000 innocent victims of a multitude of religions were massacred in the space of just a few minutes. However modern or sophisticated we might think we have become as we embark on the twenty-first century, some of our worst primeval instincts are powerfully with us still.

In this chapter, we will look briefly at two things.

The first is a personal introduction to this theme. Mine is not an academic textbook, with footnotes and quotations from original source material, but an attempt to explain one of the most complex and vital issues to intelligent lay people today. In order for me to do this it is important for you, the reader, to know where I come from, especially as I am aiming to make my views clear and to achieve a proper balance, both at the same time.

Second, we ought to look at the original faith statements of the two major protagonists in this book—Christianity and Islam. What is the Christian concept of a "just war"? Is such a thing even possible? What is jihad—is it always violent or can it be, as many Muslims are now saying, something altogether peaceful and internal? We will, deliberately, consider conflicts other than just Muslim/Christian, but need also to know a bit more about what those two faiths are supposed to believe, before we examine how they have been at daggers drawn for nearly 1,400 years.

In as much as possible of what follows, I will aim to be as fair and objective as possible. My reason is not to have some kind of woolly neutrality, since I would argue that such a goal, while praiseworthy, is in fact impossible. All humans have prejudices, and to me, at least, the real difference is whether we admit them openly or, rather, pretend that I am objective, you are prejudiced, and they are ignorant fanatics. Scholars and other writers who claim to be so wonderfully objective almost always give themselves away in some form or another, and it is surely better to admit to common human frailty from the outset, and then do one's best at least to be as fair as possible when considering those whose viewpoints differ so much from one's own.

So like most inhabitants of the West, and certainly those who would claim to be civilized, I must state at the outset that I am naturally against extremism and violence in all its forms. To me, terrorism cannot be justified, however righteous the cause; for instance, while I am of Protestant Scottish-Irish stock, I have always opposed the use of force in Northern Ireland as being against all I believe in and stand for. Democracy, not the gun, is the way to settle tribal disputes.

In being actively religious (in my case, membership of that rare beast, an actually thriving Church of England congregation in Britain), I am very much in the minority so far as Western Europe is concerned, especially in being also university educated. As will probably be obvious, I come from that part of contemporary Protestantism that regards conversion growth or peaceful missionary endeavor as the way in which the Christian faith should spread, and not the sword, or colonial conquest. (My maternal ancestors are Welsh; the English first invaded Wales and then, from 1536 to 1999, abolished the right of Welsh people to rule themselves.) Inevitably, this makes a difference to my view of the Crusades.

My kind of Christianity also believes in what the old Puritans would describe as original sin, the idea that by nature none of us are good, or capable of perfection, but that left to ourselves we instinctively do what is wrong. Far from thinking that this is a pessimistic view of life, I tend to hold that it is simply realistic, from the tantrums of small children to the much bigger horrors we see daily in the newspapers or by observing the world around us.

I do not, therefore, feel the need to defend what those who profess the same faith as I do, have done down the centuries, since they are all sinners, too. This affects not just my view of the Crusades, but also of the wars of religion that occurred in Europe as a result of the Protestant Reformation. Being paternally Northern Irish, and from a family that employed Catholics and Protestants alike on merit, whatever our own devout Protestant beliefs, I have been raised with a dislike of sectarian conflict, and an inability, despite my Calvinist theology, to wear the color orange. Christians have killed other Christians since the decision of the Emperor Constantine to convert to Christianity in the fourth century, something of which I strongly disapprove and which, whatever one's faith, should certainly not be swept under the carpet when one thinks of the many misdeeds of other religions.

One benefit of being British is, I trust, that I will be neutral in the culture wars of the United States, something that I find so often warps what even the most learned of authors write when it comes to the religious issues at the heart of this book. Just before writing this introduction, I read two fascinating books on the perennially thorny issue of jihad, a term used variably for the struggle to be a good Muslim, or, in the case of others, to wage war against those of other faiths. Is Islam naturally and instinctively a religion of peace? Or is it, by contrast, a faith with violence at its core, one that has been such since its origins over 1,300 years ago? One book argued firmly for the former view, the second for the latter, and the two respective volumes provided the quotations with which this chapter started.

One of the problems that I have observed is that, all too often, analysis of the Muslim past is determined by what side an author is on in very contemporary twenty-first-century culture war debates: either all Muslims secretly do believe in violent religious warfare, and in killing infidels on a grand scale; or Islam is overwhelmingly a peaceful faith, and the misdeeds of some rather misguided Muslims in centuries past does not really matter and should be taken in the context of living in more benighted and primitive times.

Such views naturally contradict each other! Both of them also incorrectly color the past with what we think particular groups believe today. Yet we recognize—or at least I hope we do—that Christians do not, for example, behave now as they did in the sixteenth century, when one group of believers would burn another at the stake. Religions are not absolute objects. In our own times, Islam is undergoing a major change: for the first time in Islamic history, such an enormous proportion of Muslims are living outside the Realm of Belief, the Dar al-Iman, that their faith cannot help but be affected, to literally take a more worldly view.

So if most Muslims today—and opinion polls would support this—believe that their faith is indeed one of peace, I see no reason why we should reject their sincerity. Muslim leaders such as the late Sheikh Badawi in Britain, and the happily still living Akbar Ahmed in the United States, have to me striven genuinely for peace and reconciliation.

But that does not mean that we should reinterpret the violence of the past in the light of the peace-loving present. There is something ridiculous to me about well-meaning writers glossing over the more bloodthirsty elements of Islamic history because we want, as we should, to be friendly and inclusive toward Muslims living in the West today. Such authors—Karen Armstrong, to take just one well-known example—never give the same leeway to the many atrocities in the Christian past, almost certainly because Christianity, being the majority faith of Western culture, is for them a source of criticism not of admiration.

Let us face it—for centuries, practicing Christians, Muslims, Jews, Hindus, and members of many other faiths, have all committed the most appalling deeds in the name of their particular religious faith. Not only that, but they have often done so regardless of what their founding faith documents and teachers have proclaimed is the correct way in which to live. The slaughtering of Muslims in Jerusalem in 1099 and Srebrenica in 1995 is hardly compatible with the command of Christ to love your neighbor as yourself, or to reject violence in the name of the Prince of Peace. Likewise, Muslims, for over a millennium, from the seventh to the seventeenth centuries, embarked on imperial conquest and domination, in the name of Islam, and that surely is every bit as much colonialism as the kind perpetrated by Westerners in the nineteenth and twentieth centuries. If it was wrong for Britain to conquer large swaths of Africa, it was wrong for eight-century Muslim armies to conquer Spain.

So much ink, all contradictory, has been spilled over the subject of jihad that this vexing subject has become, if anything, even more confused than before. Many contemporary writers talk about two kinds of jihad: the lesser, or military version; and the greater, or religious one that speaks about the inner struggle toward holiness. Ask most Muslims in the West today about which version they choose, they will almost invariably select the latter. But, for example, read many a work with the word *jihad* in that title and you will gain the impression that *jihad* always means violence, bloodshed, and warfare, and, especially since 2001, holy war against the West.

So what should we believe, given the contradictory evidence? Do we believe, for example, John Esposito's books, propagating a sympathetic and almost apologetic version of Islam, past and present, or the hostile and conspiracy oriented view of Robert Spencer, author and founder of the Web site Jihadwatch.org?

Thankfully, 2005 saw the publication, by the University of California Press, of *Understanding Jihad* by Rice University professor David Cook. (It could of course be the case that my enthusiasm for this particular work exists because Cook's views so closely parallel my own.) While I might be more inclined to give *contemporary* Muslims the benefit of the doubt in the interpretation of twenty-first-century jihad, nonetheless, I think that Cook makes out superbly the *historical* understanding of mainstream Islam and consequently of what *jihad* is and entails.

Melding my views with those of Cook, I would say that while it is true that most Muslims today interpret *jihad* in the sense of the struggle for inner righteousness — my own Muslim friends and colleagues, and many recent opinion polls would back this up — historically *jihad* has meant one thing and one thing only: war in the name of Allah.

This of course does not and should not mean that most Muslims around today, and certainly those living in the West, would ever see it that way *now* themselves. When some American- or British-based imam says that today Islam is a religion of peace, I see no reason why we should disbelieve him; I am not a conspiracy theorist, or one to think that supposedly peace-oriented Muslims are secretly out to kill us. Those who do hate the West and all its works, and who follow the extremist, murderous *salafiyya* form of Islam (of which more in the last chapter) are usually explicit enough in what they think of us and why.

However, to read present-time peaceful Islam back into the past is, to me as well as to Professor Cook, sheer anachronism. While, like me, he much admires the work of University of Edinburgh historian Carole Hillenbrand, for instance, on what Muslims thought of the Crusades both then and since, he points out that there is simply no written evidence that Muslims adopted a predominantly peaceful view of jihad in the way that she states. (Cook makes the same point of the numerous works of Georgetown professor John Esposito, cited earlier.)

We will look in much more detail at the actual history of early Islam in chapter 3. But first, we need a framework within which to interpret events.

My own take is that Islam is undergoing a process of change, particularly among Muslims living outside of the traditional Islamic world, in states under non-Islamic rule. Some younger Muslim men are, if anything, becoming *more* aggressive, as evidenced by the British-born and -raised Islamic terrorists of 7/7 (July 7, 2005) and those found guilty of attempted atrocities in the United Kingdom since then. However, by contrast, many other Muslims, especially women, are moving in the opposite direction, toward accommodation with the West, yet without in any way giving up their Islamic spiritual beliefs and values. Islam, in other words, is not static in all places or even within the same generation.

But as for the past, it is hard to disagree with the overwhelming historical case made by Cook's *Understanding Jihad*, not to mention similar works, some written for a more academic audience, by experts such as Rudolf Peters and Reuben Firestone. It could be that these writers also have a political agenda behind what they say, but if they do I have not found it. What Cook demonstrates conclusively is that the distinction between the greater and lesser jihad is itself anachronistic, and certainly the current-day split between the peaceful and aggressive forms is entirely modern. Jihad as traditionally understood and practiced by hundreds of years of Islam has always been primarily an expression of warfare; and the internal-struggle aspect, while real, is as often as not linked to inner preparation for outward military action.

Jihad has, therefore been part of Islam since the very beginning, even if, as Firestone shows, the actual doctrines relating to holy war took time to evolve. As several writers put it, with Sunni Islam, the gates of new or personal interpretation, or *ijtihad*, were closed in the tenth century, with reinterpretation being effectively banished since around 900. Most Islamic commentary on jihad, therefore, even if written after that time, such as the commentaries of the famous Muslim philosopher Averroes (Ibn Rushd), is more to do with the details—in the case of Averroes, for instance, making it very clear that Islam does not agree with killing women and children, a point that countless Muslims reminded the world of after the atrocities of 9/11.

Islam, as I hope to prove, is a faith in which "church and state" are by definition permanently enmeshed, with none of the sacred/secular divide that has characterized, say, Christianity since the late seventeenth/early eighteenth centuries, not to

mention Christianity's first three hundred years as a banned, illegal, underground, and persecuted faith. One of the very
reasons why Muslims in the West are turning either, in the minority, to extreme violence, and, in the majority, to peaceful accommodation, is precisely because they are, for the first time,
having to live as Muslims in a non-Islamic society.

In the past, however, this was not the case, and that is why,
I would argue, the predominant meaning of *jihad* within the Islamic world has changed.

In the past, faith and state were inexorably interlinked, and,
as Andrew Wheatcroft reminds us in his superb *Infidels*, the Ottoman Empire believed in permanent expansion, and thus in
continuous enlarging of the borders of Islam.

Today, as both surveys of Muslims and the writings of eminent Islamic peace activists such as Akbar Ahmed demonstrate,
Sufi, or mystical, Islam is overwhelmingly peaceful, contempla-
tive and nonviolent. However, Cook shows from both their
writings and their actions that this was far from the case, with
eminent Sufi leaders in the past, such as the medieval al-
Nuwayri, taking part in battle, in addition to Muslim rulers of
more martial bent. Sufis, in centuries gone by, have been as militaristic in their interpretation of jihad as anyone else, even if,
like al-Ghazali, the great philosopher, they put more emphasis
on the inner rather than violent version.

So while the many Sufi orders, from the Balkans to northern Africa, practiced the inner jihad, Muslims of all descriptions were involved as soldiers in the martial version, that of
conquest. Islam was, in effect, perpetually on the march, conquering new territory from 632 to 1683, a period more than a
millennium long. The predominance of the West is incredibly
recent, and if nations such as China or India catch up with us
during the twenty-first century, Western hegemony will be seen
as a transient phase lasting not much longer than four hundred
years, well under half the time scale of Islamic supremacy. Come
a hundred years from now, both Western and Islamic domina-

tion will both be phenomena of the past, as we continue in what might well be the Asian Millennium.

ISLAM'S WARS OF CONQUEST: THE MUSLIM EMPIRE 632—751

"Who started it?"

How often has an irate teacher or parent entered a room in which two children are fighting with each other, only for each child to blame the other one for starting the quarrel.

It is somewhat the same scenario with the age-old dispute between Christianity and Islam. Back in 1998, one thousand years after the start of the First Crusade, a group of Christian pilgrims walked the original Crusader route from France to Jerusalem, in apology for the Crusades of a millennium earlier. Even today, when debates take place between Christians and Muslims, one of the first things that the Islamic side of the discussion will do is to ask the Christians to apologize for the Crusades.

All this has done is to perpetuate what is in fact untrue — that the West is responsible for aggression against the Islamic world, and that Muslims throughout history have been the hapless victims of Christian-inspired Western imperialism.

This, in turn, ties in with two major strands of thought: first, that of self-loathing by many of my fellow intellectuals in the West, in particular those who are motivated by a strong dislike of religion of any kind; and, second, by extremist Islamic groups for whom any attempt or opportunity to tarnish the West, especially its imperialism, is always welcome. As I was writing this book, al Qaeda's number two leader, al-Zawahiri, issued a statement roundly condemning what he regarded as a Crusader and Zionist alliance against the Muslim world, i.e., those living in Lebanon and who are under Israeli attack.

What is significant about such beliefs is that millions believe in them, well beyond those writing and speaking in the two previous categories: Western secular intellectuals and Islamic hard-line religious extremists. I think Victor Davis Hanson is right, in *Between War and Peace,* to say that often people simply do not learn such things at school; and lest non-American readers feel complacent, I have found this among pupils on both sides of the Atlantic.

One of the main tasks I want to accomplish in this book is to show that this is, in fact, a wholly false perspective. In the near fourteen hundred years in which Christians and Muslims have been living side by side, there is, in reality, very little to choose between them when it comes to wars of aggression or of imperial intent. Not only that, but for the first millennium, roughly from 632 and the death of Muhammad, right up until the second attempt by the Ottoman Turks to capture the city of Vienna in 1683, the boot was firmly on the Islamic foot, with the Muslim powers on the offensive and those of Christianity on the defensive.

Although the motives of the Crusaders were often spiritual rather than imperialistic, their actions were—with some similarity to Sheikh Badawi's post-9/11 observation—quite contrary to the foundational tenets of Christian faith. To attack Christianity for the Crusades is therefore historically and theologically mistaken, even by the standards of the "just war" theory that evolved in the Church after it became the official religion of the Roman Empire in the late fourth century.

All this debate—indeed much of the subject matter of this book—is, alas, also part of the internal culture wars in the present-day United States, something wearily familiar to many American readers, and also a debate that frequently baffles those living outside it, including often-bewildered British regular visitors like me.

It is therefore important for me to say here—as someone who has close friends on both sides of the cultural conflict in the USA—that I will attempt to write as someone neutral in internal American discussions, and that what follows should be read without bias in that regard. Muslims are often perceived in stark terms, as all wonderful, peace-loving victims of Western oppression, or evildoers in whom no good is ever to be found, enemies of the West and everything we stand for. (I am exaggerating but, in the light of some books I have read on each side, sadly not by all that much.) Thankfully, too, there are plenty of historians who, while having strong views of their own, are scrupulously fair to all standpoints, and I will do my best to be the same.

So let us transport ourselves back to the seventh century, to see what happened then, regardless of whether we think that twenty-first-century Muslims are nearly all peaceful people who love us or fanatics out to blow Western civilization into oblivion.

Whatever our views on the advice Princeton sage Bernard Lewis played in advising the Bush administration in 2003 on the invasion of Saddam Hussein's Iraq, I think that his views on the contrast between early Christianity and the dawn of Islam are incontrovertible. Christianity, he shows in his many books, spent its first three hundred years as an underground, persecuted religion. Islam, from the beginning, was a faith of military and political power, with its founder, Muhammad, not just the spiritual leader, but the head of state and army commander all rolled into one.

This difference, Lewis argues, makes all the difference even today, in how those of us in the West perceive life and issues in a way quite distinct from those inspired by Islam. This will be crucial for our understanding of the final chapter, when we look at Islamic-inspired terrorism, but its application to the subject of the present topic—the historical Islamic wars of conquest— is obvious.

Islam is, and always has been, a religion of *power*. There is surely no doubt that the early Muslim centuries are those of

political and military conquest, and what controversial British/
Israeli academic Ephraim Karsh calls in his latest book, those
of *Islamic imperialism*.

While the first century of Christianity saw martyrdoms, of
converts being thrown to the lions in the Circus, or used as
human torches by the emperor Nero, the first generation of
Muhammad's followers were engaged in creating one of the
biggest land empires that the world has ever seen. From 632,
the year of his death and the election of Abu Bakr, as his first
successor or *caliph*, until exactly a century later, when, in 732,
the Muslim invaders of France were checked at a battle between Tours and Poitiers by the army of Charles Martel, the Islamic shock troops conquered an empire far bigger even than
that of Rome at its peak. From the Atlantic coast of Spain in
Europe, across the whole of North Africa and the Middle East,
through to Persia and the borders of the Indus in what is now
India: all this was under the rule of the caliphs, and under the
banner of the Prophet Muhammad and his law.

Christianity also spread in its first century, but slowly and
clandestinely, since to be caught promoting or practicing this
faith could involve death. As a result, the growth was through
conversion—through persuasion—and in the teeth of opposi-
tion from the ruling authorities.

Islam, to be fair, later also grew through a mix of trade and
conversions, especially in what is today the biggest Muslim nation in the world, Indonesia. We must never forget that most
Muslims are not Arabs, and that for them the actual language
of the Quran is as foreign to them as it is to us. Even now, for
instance, while the millions of Christians in Nigeria read the
Bible in their own language, the only permitted version of the
Quran remains that of the Arabic original—although Islam,
like Christianity, is a universal monotheistic missionary faith, it
remains rooted in its Middle Eastern origins in a way that
Christianity is not.

As British scholars Peter Cotterell and Peter Riddell remind us, this is in itself part of the military triumph of early Islam, when Islam was a both a faith and a tool of Arab imperialism, religious belief traveling hand in hand with the sword.

Debates rage among the politically correct on the one hand and the overtly incorrect on the other, as to how the early Muslim soldiers behaved. Were there massacres, with the innocent slain, or was it a more civilized affair, with casualties limited to those on the field of battle?

The problem is that by now, with so little written down at the time, it is impossible to tell. Furthermore, contemporary accounts would all be partisan one way or the other, with independent corroboration hard to achieve.

But what we do know is that the heartlands of Christianity were conquered within decades of the launch of the invasions, many of them taking place in the reign of the second caliph, Omar (634–644),

Under his rule, the Byzantine Empire suffered a major defeat at the Battle of Yarmuk in 636. By 638, Jerusalem itself was taken, and, by 641, Egypt also soon found itself under Islamic rule.

It is only the plight in twenty-first-century Iraq of the hundreds of thousands of Assyrian Orthodox and Chaldean Catholic Christians, now being harassed for their faith by extremists, that we remember at all that in the seventh century the vast bulk of the inhabitants of the Middle East were once Christian, not Muslim.

Some of the local inhabitants were glad to see the Islamic conquerors. When, in 381, Christianity became the official religion of the East Roman—or Byzantine—Empire, theologically heterodox forms of the faith were regarded as politically as well as spiritually rebellious. Such forms of dissent were thus suppressed or otherwise discouraged, in a way that was to continue in Christianity until the seventeenth century, when the results from the split caused in Western Christian faith by the Reformation led some of its adherents to return to the nonstate origins of Christianity's founders. As a result, several small Christian groups, in the seventh century, realized that Islam did not distinguish doctrinally between one form of Christianity and another, so that believers in what the Byzantines deemed to be heresies would no longer be persecuted for their beliefs. Now the Byzantine folly would haunt the Orthodox Church, since many territories formerly under its sway would be lost to Islam for good.

Rather than try to hold onto the entire Middle East, the Byzantines decided to protect their own territorial heartland — their lands in Anatolia, and their possessions in Europe and other parts of the Mediterranean. Crucially, as relates to the later Crusades, this entailed *not* attempting to reconquer areas such as Syria, Palestine and Egypt. Consequently these were to enter what Muslims before or since call the Dar al-Islam, or Realm of Islam, territory that, theologically speaking, once Muslim is always Muslim, for all time.

(Those of us outside Islam live in the Dar al-Harb, or Realm of War. Some Muslims, historically, have allowed for a Dar al-Sulh, or Realm of Truce, where non-Islamic rulers live peacefully with their Muslim neighbors, so long as that is agreeable to the Islamic side. Today, peace activists within Islam also want to create a Dar al-Salaam, which we have seen means a Realm of Peace.)

To the east, the great Iranian Empire, that of the Sassanid Persians, was also swiftly conquered. At the end of the 650s that, too, was under Muslim rule. The ancient, pre-Christian Zoroastrian faith was all but wiped out (that religion barely exists today, observed by a comparatively small number of Parsis in India, and some other scattered adherents.)

After not very long, major differences arose within the Islamic community of the faithful, the *umma*.

According to such scholars as Michael Cook (author of *The Koran: A Very Short Introduction*, and Patricia Crone, it is hard at this distance to work out who exactly believed what, when, and why. It is possible that Islamic doctrine was not fixed as early as Muslim scholarship would have us believe, though, as I have argued in other books that I have written on this area, there is no intrinsic reason to doubt the official version of the development of Islam in these early decades, so long as one does not examine it all through rose-tinted spectacles that deny the downside as well as the achievements.

Whichever side is true, the new faith found itself at war almost immediately, in armed conflict over what Muslims now call *ridda* (apostasy, the renunciation of an old faith). Only Abu Bakr, of the four Rashidun, or Rightly Guided Caliphs (632–61) died peacefully in his bed—all the others met violent ends in one form or another.

Much of the bloodshed involved who should legitimately succeed Muhammad as the leader of the faithful, the *umma*. Muhammad, as the founding Prophet, was deemed to be God's final revelation, and was, in that respect, irreplaceable. But he was also a political and military leader, since Islam then and since does not make the separation of the spiritual and the secular that early Christianity made, and that we in the West rediscovered in the seventeenth century and after.

On three occasions, Ali, who was both Muhammad's cousin and also the husband of the Prophet's daughter Fatima, was passed over as caliph. In view of his somewhat lackluster performance when he was finally chosen, this is perhaps not surprising. No daughter could succeed Muhammad. But Ali and Fatima had sons, and these were male descendants of the founder. A strong minority thus saw Ali as having all the right hereditary and spiritual credentials. Ali's supporters were the party of Ali, the Shia't Ali, and it is from them that Shia Islam and its Shiite followers—today about 15 percent of Muslims worldwide—gain their name.

Since politics and military rule were all interwined, the issue was solved by war, one group of Muslims against another. By 657 Ali had entered a truce called by Muawiya, Othman's nephew, and also governor of Damascus. Like his uncle Muawiya was a member of the Ummayad clan, the aristocratic Meccan group that had initially rejected Muhammad.

This truce was not acceptable to a group of hard-line Muslims, now called the Kharajites (literally "those who withdraw"). Although they were not influential in mainstream Islam, the Kharajites, with their purist view of how the Muslim world should be run, nevertheless continued to be highly thought of by a steady minority of extreme Muslims over the centuries. Although it might be pushing a point, one can see in them the future germ of al Qaeda and that group's equally purist view of an ideal Islamic caliphate. It was a Kharijite that murdered Ali in 661 —this in itself shows the degree of internal violence that was endemic in the Islamic world at this time.

War in the Muslim world continued; upon Ali's assassination, this time the Ummayads left nothing to chance: Muawiya proclaimed himself caliph, making his capital Damascus.

Needless to say, this assumption of power by one of the Meccan aristocracy was not acceptable to all, and fighting continued among different factions all eager to assume power of what was now an increasingly large empire, stretching from what is now Iran in the east to even further stretches of North Africa in the west.

Ali's first son by Fatima, Hassan, was not a natural warrior, and allowed the new regime to take power. But Hassan's brother Hussein was made of sterner material. When Yazid, Muawiya's son, took over as caliph in 680, many regarded what was now an hereditary monarchy in all but name as contrary to custom, as the Ummayads were not of the Prophet's family. Hussein therefore made a bid for power and was completely crushed at the Battle of Karbala that year, his head sent to the new caliph in Damascus.

Most Muslims continued to support the victorious Ummayads, and mainstream Sunni Islam does so today. But Hussein's death was seen as martyrdom by his loyal band of followers, and that remains the case with modern-day Shiite Muslims. The annual festival of Ashura, when Shiite Muslim men scourge themselves with chains, is still the major celebration of Shiite Islam in our own time. Not only that but the sense of being martyrs, of being a minority within Islam, arguably gives Shiism a very different outlook and self-image than that of the Sunni majority.

While Muslims were killing each other back in the beginning of the eighth century, they were also spreading the Dar al-Islam ever wider. By now the borders of the Indus were being reached in the east, and, by 711, most of North Africa was also in their hands.

At this stage it is important to say that most of the peoples they conquered were not forcibly converted to Islam. Arabs remained small minorities in the new domains, often restricting themselves to new garrison towns, from which they could control their territories.

Some subject peoples did convert but, under the Ummayads, who held onto power until 750 (when most of them were massacred), real authority and status belonged to the tiny Arab overlord class, similar in many ways to the equally tiny British elite who ruled over India in the days of the Raj. These converts, Muslim but not Arab, were called *mawalis* and most of them, especially those from Persia, were bitter about their second-class status.

Christians, Jews, and others deemed to be of monotheistic faith who did not convert were known as *dhimmi*, or peoples of the Book, granted special but nonetheless subservient status by the Quran, In recent years, mainly due to the pseudonymous author Ba't Yeor, the precise status of the *dhimmi* class under Muslim rule has become one of considerable debate, not just in academic circles but also in the way in which Islam has become part of the culture wars in the United States since 2001.

As a consequence it is hard to know who is right, and how exactly *dhimmi* were treated. I tend to think that their treatment varied enormously both geographically and chronologically, some Islamic rulers being highly enlightened—such as the Ummayad rulers of Andalus in Spain—whereas others being viciously oppressive, not hesitating to murder those of their subjects who refused to conform. In other words, generalization is impossible, as local circumstances vary.

One of the reasons why conversions were not forced is that non-Muslims had to pay a special poll tax. This meant that it was financially beneficial to the community for the *dhimmi* to *not* convert, as becoming Muslims eventually exempted them from the tax. So it was several centuries before the region that we now think of as inexorably Muslim actually turned to the Islamic religion. Even today the Middle East has large Christian minorities, most notably the Copts in Egypt.

By 711, Islamic armies were poised on the edge of Europe. A local dispute in Vandal-ruled Spain—Vandals being the Germanic tribe that had conquered the Iberian Peninsula after the fall of Rome—gave Tariq, an ambitious Muslim general, the chance that the invaders needed to cross over into Europe and begin what soon turned out to be yet another story of lightning conquest and Islamic triumph.

The peninsula was overrun in no time and, by the early 730s, Muslim armies were in southern France, not all that far from Paris. It seemed as if Western Europe itself would be the next victim of holy war.

However, in France, in Charles Martel, the mayor of the palace to the nominal French kings, the Merovingians, the forces of Islam had finally met their match after one hundred years of effortless conquest. In 732, a century after the death of Muhammad, at a battle somewhere between the modern towns of Tours and Poitiers, the Islamic invaders were defeated and the Frankish forces prevailed. France was safe and so was the rest of Western Europe.

Edward Gibbon, the great British eighteenth-century historian, wondered how life would have been different had that battle gone the other way. Would the Islamic scholars of Oxford have been expounding the Quran, instead of the Christian clergy upholding the Bible there instead? It is an interesting counterfactual question, and, as Gibbon also outlined in the same paragraphs, it shows how close the West came to conquest, since, as he put it, the rivers of Western Europe were surely no greater a natural barrier to invaders than were those of the Middle East and North Africa.

The Islamic conquests did not stop altogether, though. In 751, Islamic soldiers won a major battle over Tang dynasty forces at Talas, in Central Asia, expanding the Muslim conquests there with consequences we shall see in the next chapter. In 831, Muslim armies also conquered Sicily, which was not fully liberated until 1091, and the fact that the latter date is very close to that of the proclamation of the First Crusade in 1095 is surely no coincidence.

(Sicily was to be multicultural for centuries after liberation, especially under its subsequent German Hohenstaufen rulers, and through that, a major conduit of wholly positive Islamic learning in medicine, science, and similar fields in the twelfth century—we should not forget that there were some Islamic invasions, in this case of advance learning, that were entirely beneficial.)

From Sicily, occasional Islamic raiding parties were able to seize parts of southern Italy, albeit temporarily, and raiders from North Africa—later to be nicknamed the Barbary pirates—were able to spread terror on successful slaving expeditions to all parts of Western Europe, Britain included, until finally destroyed by the Americans under Thomas Jefferson as recently as the nineteenth century.

As for Spain, the liberation of the peninsula took until 1492, well over seven hundred years after it was first captured by the invaders from northern Africa. Although the Christians were able to gain as far south as Toledo by 1085, it was an immensely slow process.

In 750, yet another sanguinary coup occurred within Islam, when the Ummayads were overthrown—one of them escaped to Spain to establish his dynasty there in Andalus—and relatives of Muhammad, the Abbasid dynasty, seized power. They were to rule in Baghdad at least in name, until 1258. In terms of civilization, this was to be the golden age of Islam, when the Abbasid caliphate enabled the world of Islam to be one of the greatest intellectual power houses on earth, with discoveries in science, medicine, and philosophy that were to change history and be to the long-term good of mankind. In Spain, especially under the Ummayads, one can make a claim that there really was interreligious tolerance, since in the Iberian Peninsula—unlike, say, Egypt or what is now Iraq, where most inhabitants eventually did become Muslim—the ancestors of today's Spaniards and Portuguese remained firmly Christian.

Nevertheless, we cannot get away from the fact that all these parts of the Dar al-Islam were so because of conquest, and that while there was no compulsion to convert to Islam, nonetheless the political as well as religious leadership by Muslim caliphs was secured by these military invasions and not by the consent of the people over whom they ruled.

All this goes, I think, to prove the point made by American historians such as Thomas Madden and Victor Davis Hanson, that we need to rethink how we see the traditional strife between Islam and Christianity. Because in the past two centuries or more the West has been significantly ahead, and because in the nineteenth and twentieth centuries it was undoubtedly the West that was the conquering colonial power, we forget that for most of history it has in fact been in reverse—the Muslims were the conquerors and the Christian West was on the permanent defensive.

Although I don't buy the idea that the Crusades were no different, say, from the Normandy invasions of 1944 to liberate France, nonetheless, looked at in the long perspective, there is no doubt that, from 632 to 1683, the Islamic world was the imperial power, and the countries of Europe, from Spain to Greece, were the objects of its imperialism.

Where I differ from such historians as Ephraim Karsh, the author of *Islamic Imperialism*, is on whether such imperialism is endemic in Islam in all places and for all time. While some extremists of the al Qaeda variety certainly hold such ideas today, I do think that it is fair to argue that this is not the case, because so many millions of Muslims, for the first time, no longer live under Islamic rule, but in the West and, indeed, many are not themselves Arab. However undeniably bad the past—and some of the present—I do think that the twenty-first century might see a major shift within Islam, and, we can all hope, this will be very much for the better.

But as for the era of Islamic invasions, especially in the period of effortless conquest between 632 and 831, from the death of the Prophet to the seizure of Sicily, invasion, and the militaristic form of jihad surely prevailed. It is in that context that we ought now to go on to the Crusades, and the attempts of Western Christians to conquer the lands seized by Islam in the seventh century.

❧ 2 ❧

THE CRUSADES

"DEUS LO VEULT!" God wills it! With a great cry of assent, the crowd at the Council of Clermont in southern France roared their approval of Pope Urban II's request to launch a war against the evil forces occupying the Holy Land. And so, in 1095, the Crusades had begun.

Or is it that simple?

We have just seen that when it comes to Holy War, or jihad, the wars between Muslims and Christians had in fact begun with the Islamic invasions of 632 onward, including the invasion of the present day Middle East, North Africa, and Spain by the armies of the new caliphates. So there had been centuries of Christian/Muslim armed conflict, but begun centuries before, and begun not by Christians but by the Islamic invaders of what had up until that time been overwhelmingly Christian territory.

Also vital to remember is that the Christians of the Iberian Peninsula—no such state as Spain officially existed until 1492—had been in continuous war with different Moorish armies to liberate their lands from foreign rule since the successful Islamic invasion of 711. By the time that Urban II proclaimed his Crusade in 1095, Spaniards had been at war off and on with the Muslims of Andalus for nearly four hundred years. (And when the pope asked Christians to go to Palestine, he specifically exempted soldiers from what we now call Spain and Portugal, as they were at war with the enemy already.)

Finally, the idea of Frankish knights in the Holy Land was not even Urban's original idea. The original plea had in fact come from the Byzantine emperor, Alexius Commenus. A large Byzantine army had been routed in a decisive battle in the Anatolian town of Manzikert in 1071. The forces of Romanos IV were convincingly defeated by the invading army of the Seljuk Turk leader, Alp Arslan, and the Anatolian peninsula, which, until then had been part of the Christian Byzantine Empire since its foundation over seven hundred years before, was now in the hands of Muslim Turks. The whole balance of power in Asia Minor and the Middle East was completely and irrevocably changed by this battle. Anatolia is both Turkish and Muslim to this very day.

So the idea that the Crusades were part of a wicked conspiracy by the imperialist West to attack the peaceful, innocent land of Islam is very far from the truth.

So, too, is the notion that Christianity and holy war are compatible. Christians, according to both the Bible and the later theory of "just war," are entitled to self-defense. Wars of aggression are quite another matter, and although the casuists of the time came up with all sorts of rationales as to why an attack on the Holy Land was all right, it is certainly not how we would interpret such moral issues today. The Crusades, then, are not quite as simple as either their defenders or opponents would have us believe. No one was truly innocent.

It is interesting that in even so useful a series for the popular market as the *Complete Idiot's Guide*, that their book on the Crusades hardly mentions anything that happened before 1095, which is surely to distort the picture. Here I would agree again with writers such as Victor Davis Hanson, that we cannot really understand the story of the Crusades unless we consider the entire historical context in which they happened.

In 751, in one of the remotest parts of the world, in Central Asia, came the first of two major battles that influenced the course of history, and which are virtually unknown in the West. This was the Battle of Talas, fought near Ferghana, between an invading Islamic army and the forces of the Chinese Tang dynasty. Talas was situated at the furthest reaches of the Tang Empire, and so the fact that they lost is not surprising. But their loss was to have a major long-term impact that, just three hundred years later, was to change Europe and the Middle East forever.

Although Tang control of Central Asia was tenuous, it nonetheless existed. So long as the Tang had the military predominance in the region, they could keep an eye on the nomadic tribes that continually threatened to erupt and create mayhem over a wide area. One day, such an explosion of nomad power from the steppes would lead to Genghis Khan and the enormous Mongol Empire. Here the defeat at Talas made the difference to the fate of the many Turkic tribes inhabiting the area.

Islamic victory and Chinese defeat at Talas meant that the Turkish groupings, still pagan, came into direct border contact with the enormous Abbasid Empire, still at its peak of influence and power. Muslim missionaries brought the message of Islam, and, over the course of time, the different Turkic tribes converted to the still comparatively new religion. This in itself is important to remember. Because so much of the world was conquered by Islamic armies, we tend to forget that numerous peoples, from Central Asia all the way to West Africa and Indonesia, converted voluntarily, without the intervention of any armies. The Turkish peoples are a classic case in point.

By the end of the tenth century, two major changes had taken place. First, the Turkic nomads were on the move, in one of the biggest human migrations in history. Second, key tribes had already converted to Islam, and were ready to join their fellow Muslims in common cause. Among the most important

Turkish leaders was Seljuk, who gave his name not just to his own tribe but, in the space of just a few years, to an entire empire. Just as important, the Seljuk Turks were Sunni, followers of the mainstream of Islam, and thus no friends to the Fatimid caliphs who ruled over Egypt and much of the Holy Land itself.

In 1055, not only was the Abbasid caliphate itself comparatively powerless, but the Buyid dynasty—a Shiite family from what is now Iran—was also on its last legs. When the Seljuks invaded, they successfully captured Baghdad, deposed the heretical Buyids, and replaced them as the real rulers of the Abbasid Empire.

By 1071, just sixteen years later, the leader of the Seljuks was Alp Arslan, Seljuk's great-grandson. He had succeeded as ruler of part of modern Iran in 1059, and in 1063 he succeeded his uncle as the sultan, the Turkish name given to the official who actually controlled the Abbasid caliphate. "Alp Arslan" means "brave lion," and he was soon to prove himself a courageous and successful leader.

He had two tasks. The first was to recapture Syria from the Fatimids, whom good Sunni Muslims regarded as heretics. The Fatimids had ruled Jerusalem since 969, and this was an affront to all devout Sunnis. Second, his room for expansion was to the north of that area, the Anatolian Peninsula, and that region was, as it had been for centuries, under the control of the Christian Byzantine Empire (and its predecessor, the Roman Empire, for many years before that).

The year 1071 saw two major events. One was the brief Seljuk capture of Jerusalem, expelling the Fatimids, until the latter were able to retake Jerusalem in 1098. This is important because, as the doyen of Middle East historians Bernard Lewis reminds us, the *real* struggle in Syria/Palestine during this period was not so much the Christian/Muslim struggle but the desire of Sunni Muslims to eliminate their Shiite Muslim rivals

from power and to overthrow Fatimid rule of so much of the
Middle East.

But it was the other major event of 1071 that was to make
all the difference and, I would argue, to result in the Crusades'
happening at all. This was our second little-known but historically crucial fight, the Battle of Manzikert, between the Seljuks
under Alp Arslan and the Byzantines, under their emperor, Romanos IV (Romanus IV Diogenes).

Alp Arslan had begun his probing attacks on Anatolia in
1068. By this time, the Byzantine Empire, once so formidable
and seemingly invincible, had been riven by internal fighting and court factions—Romanos was, himself, regarded as a
usurper on the throne. Not only that but the southern branch
of the Normans—the same group that conquered England in
1066—had only just captured southern Italy from Byzantine
rule, and, with full papal blessing, liberated Sicily from two
hundred years of Islamic domination. The Byzantines were
thus obliged to fight a two-front war—against fellow Christians
(albeit Catholic) in Europe and against the Muslim Seljuks in
Asia Minor.

So by 1071, Romanos decided that it was time to deal with
the Seljuks—the invaders from the East—once and for all. He
set off with a large army, not all of whom were Byzantine regular troops. Some were Frankish soldiers from Western Europe, and others, fatally as it would prove, were ethnic Turks
hired as mercenaries. Worse still, one of the key Byzantine
commanders, Andronicas Doucas, was one of Romanos's main
rivals for power back in Constantinople.

By August, the two armies, Byzantine and Seljuk, were
near what is now Lake Van. Not all historians agree on the
exact dates of the final confrontation at Manzikert. But of the
outcome there is no doubt—it was a total disaster for the Byzantines, and for Romanos in particular, who was captured, and
then deposed as emperor by his domestic enemies. The Turkish
mercenaries defected to their ethnic kinsmen, the Seljuks, and

the troops under Doucas explicitly disobeyed orders. Arslan and the Seljuk Turks were victorious.

Arslan only lived another year. His successor, Malik Shah, died in 1092, and it was that event which unwittingly provided the West with the opportunity it needed to reconquer the Holy Land.

For after Malik's death, the once-great Seljuk Empire — nominally still under the Abbasid caliphate — began to unravel. Instead of handing it to one successor, Malik divided his realm among different members of his family, which, human nature being what it is, resulted in not one strong empire but numerous competing principalities, all vying with one another, often warring against one another, and none strong enough to defeat the major invasion that, unknown to them, was soon on its way. Without this, it is most unlikely that the Crusaders would have progressed more than a few miles, let alone been able to reach all the way to Jerusalem and set up a new kingdom.

Later on in this chapter, we will look at some of the key issues involved within Europe at that time. One of the points that cannot be emphasized enough is that the Crusades were, in essence, as much about the desire of the papacy to exert control over others within its domain as to launch attacks on people outside of it. The Crusades were as much against pagan European Lithuanians and to recapture lost Christian territory in Spain, as they were an attempt to invade the heartland of Islam by capturing Jerusalem. Tales of Richard the Lionheart and Saladin, however popular they might have become down the centuries, are, in one sense highly misleading.

In fact, one could say that a major impetus for the Crusades was the successful capture of Toledo from the Moors in 1085. Andrew Wheatcroft, in his deservedly influential work *Infidels*, suggests that the Christian liberation of Toledo by the forces of Alfonso VI was in many ways the real start of the *reconquista* of Spain by the Christian kingdoms that takes us all the way down to the final capture of Granada in 1492. While I might want to put the date of the reconquest earlier, Wheatcroft's point is an important one: people in Europe were waking up to the fact that the Islamic armies were not invincible and that real progress could be made to expel them from Christian territory.

One of the reasons why Alfonso was able to prevail is similar to the situation in the Middle East—the once-mighty Ummayad caliphate in Andalus had disintegrated at the start of the eleventh century, and no one of the successor Moorish kingdoms was powerful enough on its own to withstand an outside attack.

In fact Alfonso's victory at Toledo soon made it worse for the Christian armies, since the local Moorish rulers appealed for aid to the powerful rulers of the new Almoravid Empire in Morocco. Troops under Almoravid command quickly invaded, and soon most of Moorish-ruled Spain was ruled not from within Andalus but from Morocco, following their victory at Sagrajas in 1086. (Almoravid rule did not last too long—by the 1120s another Islamic revivalist group from North Africa, the Almohads, took over first their lands in Africa and then in Spain. But Toledo remained firmly in Christian hands.)

There was one other piece of good news for Western Christians. Bad as the Norman conquest of southern Italy had been for the Byzantines, the 1061–91 capture by the Normans of Sicily, from Islamic rule, was also a major boost to Catholic Christian morale. As Marcus Bull notes in *The Oxford History of the Crusades*, the popes were supportive of both the recapture of Christian Spain and that of Sicily, and so it is not surprising that they would soon turn their attention elsewhere.

One of the key aims of the papacy was to gain greater power within Europe, especially over Christian rulers who wanted to diminish papal strength for internal political reasons. This was as important a motive for the Crusades as the desire to regain Christian territory. But for now we will concentrate on the latter—the wish of Christians in Western Europe to recapture lands once under Christian rule, in the case of Spain and the Holy Land, and to conquer pagan kingdoms contiguous to Christian soil, in the case of the campaigns in the Baltic area and in Central Europe.

This surely, then, was all in the mind of Pope Urban II when he proclaimed what we now call the First Crusade, at Clemont, in 1095.

Because of our romanticized and thus often distorted picture of the Crusades, we tend to think that the whole of Europe responded eagerly to the request to attack the Saracens, as the Islamic rulers of the Middle East were called. Proper historical research has shown that, on the contrary, comparatively few kings, great lords, knights, and ordinary men took up the cross and set off for Palestine. Crusading was definitely a minority interest. Nor was it a case of younger sons, deprived of the ability to inherit land at home who set off for economic as well as spiritual reasons, to seek their fortune in new lands. Modern discoveries show, if anything, the opposite—that since going on a Crusade was so incredibly expensive, and burdensome on the estate, that it was in fact usually eldest sons who ventured out, since they needed all the revenue possible from their lands to be able to finance the trip.

The work of Jonathan Riley-Smith, and that of historians who agree with him, has also shown that for most Crusaders, spiritual motivation was very high on the list of reasons to go. In part this was because of the papal decision to issue indulgences—forgiveness from sins—for all those who went. But while we today, in a more cynical age, might tend to downplay this, in early medieval times this was a very considerable spiritual blessing to be granted, and it would have made a vast difference to the conscience of many a knight, that through the pope God really would forgive you your sins if you risked all to recapture Jerusalem. In a much less literate society, spirituality was frequently not a question of what you read but what you saw or did, and so works of merit, actual deeds, counted for far more then than they would for people of religious faith today. For the average Crusader, it really was a *holy* war.

The first Crusade to set out for the East has been given the misleading name of the People's Crusade, giving the false impression that it was a raggle-taggle army of ordinary folk. In fact, not a few of the soldiers were aristocratic, and Peter the Hermit, their leader, was no wild man. But, without the full backing of a major state, failure was inevitable, and the People's Crusaders were wiped out not long after they arrived in Muslim-held territory.

In 1096 the real First Crusade began. As John France reminds us, this was initially not a single army but several, all with different starting points but with the same initial destination in mind—Constantinople. Count Raymond of Toulouse, the ruler of much of southern France, was among the early leaders, as were Godfrey of Bouillon, who ruled a duchy in what is now Belgium, and his brother Count Baldwin of Boulogne; Bohemond of Taranto, one of the Normans from Sicily, and his nephew Tancred; and Duke Robert of Normandy and his cousin Robert of Flanders. This was a most impressive array of medieval leadership, but the fact that each man was used to sole command, not to sharing it with equals, did not always make for smooth decision-making when the first battles took place.

Those passing through Germany killed numerous Jews on the way. We remember this now as a distant prequel to the Holocaust. This was something that the popes opposed, and which a later preacher, Bernard of Clairvaulx, condemned zealously. But it is a major blot on the record of the Crusaders even though, once settled in Palestine, many of the later Crusaders developed much better relations with the Jews than existed back home in Europe.

We should not forget that while it was Urban II who had called the Crusade, it was, theoretically, a call to aid Emperor

Alexius against the threat of Islamic armies to his domains. Within just three years, this original goal had been forgotten; the Crusaders set up a series of counties, principalities, and a kingdom of their own. This was due, in part, to the way in which Crusaders and Byzantines were to fall out with each other. But however things turned out subsequently, they all began in Constantinople.

So much has been written about every detail of the Crusades that we need not go into the minutiae of the progress here. Suffice it to say that, by 1097, the coalition was ready to launch the offensive, and that by June they had achieved their first victory, the Anatolian city of Dorylaeum. This was important, because the route chosen was overland from Constantinople to Jerusalem, rather than trying a major seaborne assault on Palestine itself. (This would only be possible later, when key ports such as Acre had already been captured.)

By October 1097 came the first big test—the capture of the northern Syrian city of Antioch. This proved to be no easy task, and it was not until June 1098 that the city was finally captured, against considerable odds.

It was then just over another year for the actual goal of the Crusade itself: the capture of Jerusalem, the Holy City.

As is now widely known and was recorded in one medieval chronicle, the Crusaders notoriously waded ankle deep in blood when they finally took the city. Everyone was massacred. The slaughter included the local Jews and Christians as well as Muslims.

Since the Crusaders had not received the military aid they had expected from the Byzantines, they swiftly began to set up independent states of their own. The county of Edessa was the first (and also the first to be conquered, in the 1140s), next there was the county of Tripoli and the principality of Antioch. But Jerusalem was the main goal, and that was proclaimed a kingdom upon its capture in 1099.

Initially Godfrey of Bouillon was asked to be king. He refused, and was made advocate, or protector, of the holy places. But when he died in 1100, his brother Baldwin was not so bashful, and became the first king of Jerusalem.

While some of the Crusaders did stay—including a portion of those who came in a second wave in 1101—most of the knights and nobles went back to Europe, their duty to the cross having been done.

So while the four small Crusader states—known as Outremer, or "beyond the sea"—clung perilously on, they did so often without the large military resources that they would have needed to make an effective, permanent settlement and garrison in what remained a hostile environment. In the Baltic Crusades, large numbers of people eventually settled in the conquered areas, and in Spain the *reconquista* was taking lands fully inhabited by their ethnic and religious kindred. But that was not the case in Outremer, and it is therefore hard to see how it could be described as a colonial enterprise rather than a spiritual exercise in keeping holy sites under Christian control.

In 1144 came an event that was to lead to the eventual defeat of the Crusaders. While the Abbasid caliphs nominally ruled in Baghdad, we have seen that in fact real rule was by others, and that the Crusaders had been able to prevail in 1099 because their enemies were split. But with the advent of the powerful Islamic warlord Zengi (or Zangi), the *atabeg* military ruler of Mosul, the Crusaders' days were numbered. In 1144, he recaptured Edessa, the most vulnerable of the Crusader states, for Islam. Although he did not live long to see the fruits of his conquests, he had begun a process of consolidating Islamic power that finally provided the Muslims with the impetus that they needed.

Zengi's success led to the Second Crusade. Like all but the First, this was a failure so far as helping Outremer was concerned. Foreign armies came—one led by the king of France himself—and no real progress was made. Edessa remained in Islamic hands, and the kingdom of Jerusalem and the two re-

maining small states were as insecure as ever. Furthermore, the
kings were unlucky, what with uncertain succession, women rivals and their husbands, and a leper on the throne. In a feudal
society that needed a strong male to rule effectively, the kingdom of Jerusalem did not have the leadership that a precarious
medieval country required.

(Jonathan Riley-Smith was right to point out, in a British
newspaper review of the Ridley Scott movie *Kingdom of Heaven*,
that there are not a few historical inaccuracies in the film, with
several events being conflated together that were in fact years
apart.)

Zengi's Nur al-Din was made of even sterner material and,
as well as being a good general was also a devout Muslim. One
of the things that Ephraim Karsh's controversial book *Islamic
Imperialism* does prove beyond peradventure is that up to Zengi
and Nur al-Din, the Islamic countries surrounding Outremer
spent as much time attacking one another and concerned to win
local faction fights as they did in even contemplating removing
the European invaders. When Nur al-Din began his consolida-
tion and conquests, Muslims armies once again began to consider jihad, Holy War against the infidels in their midst.

It is possible writers such as Karsh are correct to put a cynical spin upon all this, and that dynastic desires were truly para-
mount. Certainly, Nur al-Din and several of the other local
Muslim rulers often did put their dynasties at the forefront of
their ambitions, but I see no reason why they could not have
been genuine in their Islamic aspirations as well—there is no
reason why faith and family should have been mutually contradictory.

Nur al-Din and his family were Turks, like most of the
other powerful Sunni magnates of the time. But they did draw
upon other races for their elite troops, and in due time one of
these, Salah al-Din, known to generations in the West simply as
Saladin, came to prominence. Saladin is interesting now not
least because he came from Tikrit, which, many centuries later,

was to be the birthplace and power base of Saddam Hussein. But although millions of Arabs have given Saladin heroic status, especially in the twentieth century, as a man who beat the wicked Westerners, Saladin was in fact a Kurd, the most famous member that that ethnic group has ever produced. (In that Kurds have endured long decades of oppression at the hand of Sunni Muslims, Saladin's iconic status among Arabs is thus ironic.)

Critics such as Karsh are fair to say that Saladin did not exactly hurry to remove the Crusader kingdoms, spending far more time building up a powerful dynasty of his own—the Abuyyids—to replace that of Nur al-Din, than invading Outremer. In 1169, notionally under Nur al-Din (who in turn was notionally under the caliph), he finally conquered the Fatimid caliphate, ending two hundred years of heretical Shiite rule over Egypt and much of the rest of the Muslim world. Here I agree very fully with the writings of Bernard Lewis, who argues convincingly that this was the *real* battle—not to rid Palestine of the pesky Christians but to purge the disgrace of a major heretical caliphate in the heartland of Islam.

Whether Saladin's prime goal in doing so was dynastic or spiritual—and I would say it is both—does not matter, in one sense. The main thing is that strategically the Crusaders were now surrounded on both sides by a powerful new Sunni Islamic combination, and that playing off Sunni Turks against Shiite Fatimids was no longer possible. (Remember that the Fatimids were not exactly sorry to see the Seljuks lose territory back in 1097–1099.)

So I think that it is legitimate to say that in military terms, as well with regard to its spiritual importance, Saladin was right to put the conquest of Egypt first, since that was the major obstacle. Whether or not it is right to say that but for the foolishness of some nobles in attacking Muslims caravans, the kingdom would have lasted, unmolested by Saladin, is another matter. I think that since Saladin was motivated by a combination of both dynastic ambition for his family and by a genuine desire to rid the area of its infidels, he would have attacked the Crusader states sooner or later.

Whichever way it might have taken place, Saladin, thanks to the foolishness of the king, Guy of Lusignan, was able to vanquish the Crusader army at the Battle of the Horns of Hattin in 1187. Jerusalem was seized not long thereafter. For a brief while in the thirteenth century it was in Christian hands again, not, as we shall see, because of military prowess but as a result of peaceful negotiation. But as for the long term, Jerusalem remained for all intents and purposes under Islamic rule until 1917.

Richard the Lionheart, the king of England, has long been thought one of the most romantic of all Crusaders. When the papacy heard of the capture of Jerusalem, a new Crusade, the Third, was launched, and Richard (notionally King Richard I of England, but in fact a ruler who never visited his domain during his entire time as king, Hollywood notwithstanding) eagerly took up the cross, at enormous financial cost to his realms in England and France (which was more of France than his fellow Crusader, King Philip, ruled himself).

Richard, while a great patron of the arts, was probably in reality one of England's least agreeable kings, with the temperament of a psychopath. I think in Britain he is popular because of the deep unpopularity of his younger brother and successor, King John, and also because of the way in which the Crusades were bathed in an aura of romance centuries after Richard had died. Be that as it may, the contest between Saladin on the one hand and Richard on the other has been seen subsequently as the embodiment of chivalry. But as Maurice Keen's definitive book *Chivalry* makes clear, such notions in fact come from a later period in the Middle Ages, and were, in any case, embellished still more in Victorian times. So while it is possible that Richard and Saladin treated each other with the utmost courtesy, as noble opponents, it is hard to know at this distance how much is true and what is in fact legend.

One thing is for certain though—like all later Crusades, the Third was a military disaster. Jerusalem was not recaptured, and the possession of the holy city was, as we saw, the real motive for all the invasions of Palestine from the West. What might be said is that Richard bought time for the rump territories that remained in Christian hands, and would do so, thanks to him, for another century to come. Not only that but, by conquering Cyprus en route to Palestine, he provided the Crusaders with their main headquarters for the next five hundred years.

Unfortunately, when he did so, he seized it from its previous Byzantine rulers, and imposed upon the majority Greek Orthodox population centuries of Catholic rule. We saw that there was little love lost between the Byzantines and Crusaders, and shortly that enmity was to become permanently much worse, to the long-term detriment of Christianity in the Levant and southeast Europe.

When the illustrious medieval Pope Innocent III declared a Crusade in 1202, officially the Fourth, he could not have realized what a devastating effect his summons would have, with terrible repercussions right down to the twenty-first century and hundreds of thousands of deaths in Bosnia in the 1990s.

Crusading was supposed to have been against the infidels, or heretics. But the Fourth Crusaders never made it to the Holy Land. Instead the greed of the Venetians, led by their old and partly blind doge, Dandolo, resulted in the Crusaders' becoming involved first in a succession dispute within the Byzantine Empire, and then with taking over the empire itself. The so-called Latin Empire lasted only until 1261, but its disastrous consequences were permanent.

The Byzantines, the one great bulwark for centuries against Islamic incursion into southeast Europe, never fully recovered, and by the time that the forces of the Ottoman Empire seized Constantinople in 1453, the empire was a mere tiny shell of its once-mighty self. Other former Byzantine territories remained under Western rule for longer; for example, the Ionian Islands, until 1798 under the Venetians, and then under the British until the 1860s. Northern Greece was not under Greek control again until 1913, within the lifetime of some alive today.

Subsequent Crusades—historians list up to nine altogether—also proved useless in regaining the Holy Land. Ironically, the one person who *did* manage to return Jerusalem to Christian rule, Holy Roman Emperor Frederick I, did so without launching an official Crusade, and, because he was an excommunicate, his success was not even recognized by the pope. After the truce that he was able to arrange following his visit went on to expire, Jerusalem was lost again, this time permanently, until 1917, when liberated by the Australians and British under General Allenby.

Several Crusades, with good cause, aimed at destroying the power of the Mamluk rulers of Egypt. Two of these involved the French king, Saint Louis (Louis IX). In the first attempt, the Crusaders can be said to have thrown away their early advantage, and the second time around, they never really managed to get all that far.

In essence, I think that the problem was the one we saw earlier: not enough European forces lived permanently in the Holy Land, and the need for outside armies from the West to come to the rescue continued. Kings, dukes, and other foreign potentates always had agendas of their own, and these did not necessarily chime with those of the king of Jerusalem and his subjects.

In fact, one could argue that it is precisely because the Crusades were *not* a colonial venture but a religious one, that they failed, as no Western state fully owned the shaky principalities that the Crusaders set up in the first wave after 1099. The new states belonged, in a real sense, to papal enthusiasm, and so it was not in the ultimate vested interest of any one Western state to see them permanently protected. Successive popes had to start afresh, with new Crusades, to rekindle the old ardor, and to persuade yet a new generation of Western rulers and their knights that the lands in which Christ had once lived were truly worth keeping in Christian hands.

This is, I think, why other Crusades—notably those in France, Spain, and in the Baltic region, succeeded. In these, impulses as strong as—if not actually stronger than—religion helped to make sure that the conquests were permanent. Spanish-speaking Christians naturally wanted to keep hold of their own country, to free their own fellow countrymen from foreign domination. The kings of France did not like the fact that so much of their nominal realm in the south—the Langue-doc—was in such chaos and outside of monarchical control from Paris. German knights wanted to extend the borders of their ethnic territories.

This is not to say that Spaniards, Frenchmen, and Teutons lacked the same degree of religious motivation that propelled people to Palestine. Far from it—the fact that the occupiers of so much of Spain were Muslim surely added a powerful incentive, since the liberation they sought was thus as much religious as territorial or nationalist. The existence of the Cathars in the Languedoc threatened the Catholic Church in Europe as well as offending the centralizing tendencies of the French kings (who were also busily engaged in trying to expel their fellow Catholics, the English, from as much of France as possible).

But from 1291 to 1917, there was no Western presence in Palestine, and then only, as such historians as David Fromkin and Ephraim Karsh argue separately, because of the folly of the Ottoman Empire in choosing the Germans rather than the British in World War I. Spain, however, was conquered, and permanently. Cathars vanished from southern France—albeit, I would argue, ultimately by the active evangelism of the new Dominican order and the terrors of the equally new institution, the Inquisition, rather than through any of the more gruesome military activities of Simon de Montfort and the Albigensian Crusaders. The Baltic States and Poland may have ethnically cleansed—to use that horrible 1990s euphemism—its Jewish inhabitants in World War II and its ethnic Germans after 1945, but the region is now firmly Christian, Catholic, and today part of both NATO and the European Union. The Teutonic Knights might have lost the military battles in the fifteenth century but, spiritually speaking, the Northern Crusades can be deemed a long-term success.

This is all something to be born in mind when we consider the Crusades *as a whole movement of Catholic Europe*, rather than just concentrate on the narrower remit of the invasion of the Middle East, which, as we know, ended in 1291 in final exile and failure. Some works on the Crusades, notably those of John France and Jonathan Riley-Smith, take their examination of Crusading as a phenomenon well beyond the end of the thirteenth century, to the conquest in 1798 of the island of Malta, the territory given to the Knights Hospitallers by Emperor Charles V in the sixteenth century, to compensate for their loss of Rhodes to the Turks.

In one sense this is surely right: one wishes, for example, that more European countries had rallied around Hungary in the late 1390s. In 1396, a major Western Christian army fought the invading Ottomans at a place called Nicopolis. It was a disaster for the Christian forces, as the Ottomans trounced them conclusively. The defeat opened the way to the domination of the Balkans by the Muslim Ottoman Turks in a way that I would argue was more important than the much better known battle of Kosovo, fought nine years earlier, between the Ottomans and the Serbs. Nicopolis's was a battle like that of Manzikert, and one, it would seem, which ended a three-hundred-year Crusading tradition by the West. This is not to say that minor land-based skirmishes ceased to take place but, after Nicopolis, the West was firmly on the defensive. Hungary was conquered in 1526, Vienna came within a hairbreadth of being seized in 1529, and, as Bernard Lewis is so correct to remind us, it was not until 1683 that the West was finally able to gain the initiative. All these Balkan disasters can, also I think, be attributed directly to the barbaric mercenary seizure by Western armies of Constantinople in 1204, which means that the Orthodox Christians of southeast Europe had to suffer between five and six hundred years of alien rule as a result, with recent consequences to which I have referred already.

One of the key themes in this chapter is that Crusades were against anyone the popes deemed to be an enemy, and not just therefore against Islam. Whenever we see twenty-first-century Islamic extremist spokesmen use the term "Crusader" *exclusively* of the Christian/Muslim struggle, they are therefore being simply historically wrong. Cathars were massacred in large numbers on the orders of Simon de Montfort, and many inhabitants of the Baltic region found themselves under alien Germanic rule up until 1945.

As for the Jewish inhabitants of many of these lands, we recall the horrors of the Riga Ghetto during the Holocaust, but forget that the fabulous Ladino Jewish civilization of Andalus, a unique flowering of learning and culture that produced giants of the stature of Maimonides, also met two sad endings: expulsion under the Catholic rulers Ferdinand and Isabella, in the fifteenth century; and then, after the Ladino-speaking Jews had fled to Greece and other Ottoman territories, in which they were not persecuted, death came all over again in the Holocaust, when former UN secretary-general Kurt Waldheim, as a young officer, was among those responsible for the mass annihilation of the centuries-old Ladino Jewish communities in a place such as Thessaloniki.

Let us therefore look at the other, equally important, and, I would argue, equally theologically blessed, Crusades in other parts of the world than the Middle East; in the north of Europe against the pagan Slavic kingdoms, in the Languedoc against the Cathar heretics, and then in Spain against the Moorish invaders of Spanish soil, the *reconquista*.

Oxford historian Eric Christensen has written, in his book *The Northern Crusades*, that everyone has heard of those that took place in Palestine, and most people who know anything about medieval history have heard about the Albigensian Crusade in southern France, against the Cathars. However, as he points out, to most of us the Crusades that took place in northern Europe, against the Wends, Livonians, and other similar Baltic tribes, are almost completely unknown.

Yet the great champion of the Second Crusade, Bernard of Clairvaulx, was also the major cheerleader behind the first of these Crusades in the Baltics, that against the Wendish tribes, proclaimed in 1147.

In many ways, the fact that what had until that date been the peaceful evangelism of the Slavic and Finnish peoples beyond the Danish/Germanic border turned into a military Crusade, with results that lasted until the Germans were forcibly evicted from much of Poland and the Baltic after World War II, is a real tragedy. Many Slavs and Finns/Estonians spent centuries under alien rule, until 1919, and a town such as Memel, founded in medieval times by German crusaders, was very nearly one of the causes of the Second World War. The legacy of conquest is a very long one.

Yet at the same time, the Lithuanians and other Baltic ethnic groups did lastingly convert to Christianity, albeit, in the case of Lithuania in 1387, without any military aid. So in one sense, therefore, the northern Crusades were a success, like the *reconquista* in Spain but unlike their more famous equivalent in the Middle East.

The first northern Crusade, against the Wends, began in 1147. Bernard, the great enthusiast for the Second Crusade in Palestine, also met with many leading German rulers, and realized that the pagan tribes beyond the borders were still unconverted and were resisting all Christian influence. He thus persuaded the pope also to launch a Crusade against the pagans on the outer reaches of Europe, and the same kind of indulgences applied to those who took up the Cross there as went to Jerusalem.

Before we look at the Crusades themselves, we need to remind ourselves how much of Europe remained pagan in the twelfth century. Although much of Western Europe had been converted as far back as Roman times, the history of the Saxon invasions of Britain should remind us that, after the fifth century, much of Europe needed converting all over again, as a reading of, for example, Bede's *Ecclesiastical History of England* demonstrates clearly. Much of Scandinavia—such as Denmark and Sweden—were Christian by the tenth century; however, large parts of northern and central Europe remained firmly pagan, with ancient tribal religion very much still in place.

Initially, as Christensen points out, the Wendish Crusade failed, certainly so far as what happened in the lifetime of Bernard is concerned—he died a disappointed man. But the impetus was taken up by two key northern Christian rulers: Henry the Lion of Saxony, and, above all, by Valdemar the Great of Denmark—the Danish cross, or Dannebrog, remaining the key component of the Danish flag to this very day. Valdemar and Henry were highly successful in their conquests, and by the 1180s considerable swaths of territory had been claimed for Christendom.

Here, as elsewhere, I agree though with the sentiments of Jonathan Riley-Smith in his many works on the Crusades. Both Bernard and the pope in 1147, and many of the bishops and similar church leaders taking part in the Crusade, had the notion that those attacked ought to be either suppressed or forcibly converted. This, as Riley-Smith reminds us, is bad theology, since it went entirely contrary to centuries of teaching in the Christian Church. Invading people was one thing, but military evangelism—something that the Crusaders in Palestine never even contemplated against Muslims—was quite another.

In the north, the Crusades now took an interesting turn. While the rulers of countries such as Denmark and Sweden (two countries which were also briefly joined into one large Scandinavian kingdom) continued onward, the real impetus now came from a Crusader order that, in a sense, ended up fighting the northern pagan tribes so as to be able to find something to do. These were the Teutonic Knights, founded in 1190 after the fall of Jerusalem, in Acre, initially to look after a hospital, and only after a few years to change into the Crusading order with which we have become familiar.

(In the case of the Teutonic Knights, they have now come full circle—the Catholic branch still exists but as a religious order, which laymen can only join as honorary members, and now with its headquarters in Austria.)

Their rule was based closely on that of the Templars, and, while like that Order and that of the Hospitallers they were theoretically open to all nations, in practice their membership was mainly Germanic—although we should here remember that no actual country called Germany as such existed.

With the fall of Jerusalem there was increasingly little for them to do in the Holy Land, the original rationale for their existence as well as that of all the similar Crusading orders. In the 1220s, they served in Hungary, fighting pagans there, but the king was suspicious that they would want to form a state of their own.

Thus, in 1225, they were asked if they would be willing to crusade against the pagans in Prussia and the Baltics, and this was to be their rationale for the next three hundred years, until the secularization of the order and the taking of its lands by its final secular rulers.

Conrad of Masovia, the ruler of a Polish principality, invited them to protect his lands against the invaders, the pagan Prussians, who had been seizing Christian ruled territory. There had been local Crusading orders, including the Knights of the Sword, which the Teutonic Knights later incorporated, but these did not have the military prowess to match their zeal (and in the case of the Sword Knights, not enough of the Christian virtues either).

Unlike the local Christian armies, the Teutonic Knights proved spectacularly successful, conquering most of the eastern part of Prussia by the end of the thirteenth century, and also much of the Baltic region as well.

Eventually the main Crusade developed against the Lithuanians, a powerful pagan nation as yet unconquered and unevangelized. Here again the Knights were successful, but this inevitably drew them into conflict with their notional allies, the Poles, who understandably felt threatened by the fact that the Teutonic Knights were creating a powerful state under their own rule, and one thus not owing allegiance to the Polish kingdom. Whereas in the Holy Land there had been official numbers of Crusades, that in northern/central Europe was deemed to be an eternal or perpetual Crusade, with the Teutonic Knights actual rulers of the countries that they had conquered, unlike the orders that had existed in Palestine.

By the end of the fourteenth century, warriors came from all over Europe to help the Teutonic Knights in their quest — one of these was the English Henry of Bolingbroke, later to become King Henry IV of the Lancastrian dynasty.

But in 1387, their rationale against the Lithuanians ended. The Lithuanian leader, Jagellio, converted to Christianity upon marrying a Polish princess. Their enemies were now a Christian country. Lithuanians, Poles, and Teutonic Knights combined to remove the one still-pagan Lithuanian tribe in 1399, but the tension between the Knights and their fellow Catholics in Poland/Lithuania now grew tense. In 1410, the Knights were overwhelmingly defeated at a battle called either Grunwald or Tannenberg. While the order continued to exist until the sixteenth century, its glory days were over.

With the Reformation they ended altogether, since Luther's

theology was not at all friendly to Crusading knights, and the once-great orders were secularized, in 1525 when Albert of Hohenzollen became a Protestant and in 1562 when the Livonian branch of the Teutonic Knights was similarly turned into a secular state. The Northern Crusades were finally over.

However, secularization brought with it, for the Prussians, union with the German principality of Brandenburg (Albert came from its ruling family). Prussia eventually became the most powerful of the Germanic states within the Holy Roman Empire, and the leading member of the German Empire after unity in 1871. Not until 1945 and German defeat in World War II were the Poles finally able to reclaim all the territory that should have been theirs, so the legacy of the Teutonic Knights and conquest by German monk soldiers over Slavic peoples lasted until our own times.

Remember—all the Lithuanians, Estonians, Latvians, and other races attacked by the Teutonic Knights were fellow Europeans. It was imperialism, and in the name of Christianity, but one group of Europeans conquered another, with repercussions down until the twentieth century.

The next Crusade of importance is called the Albigensian Crusade. Here I think that the criterion for what makes a Crusade as set out by the doyen of Crusading studies, Jonathan Riley-Smith, matches perfectly. To him, it was a Crusade if the pope said so, and there is no doubt about the full degree of papal support in the Crusade to rid the Languedoc of Cathar heretics, even though, in this instance, it was not Germans fighting Lithuanians, or Spaniards against Moors, or Frankish knights against Seljuk Turks, but one army of Frenchmen, often from the north, against fellow Frenchmen from the south.

I think that Riley-Smith is fair to say that the Crusade against the Cathars really began because conventional spiritual means—that of conversion, and peaceful evangelism—had not been working. The count of Toulouse had, the Church reckoned, been lax at expelling heresy from his domains, and it would need outside Crusading force to rid the region of the pestilence of heresy.

Strictly speaking, though, the Cathar beliefs were, I would have thought, a good deal further than heresy—say that of the Waldensians of the Alpine valleys not so far away, whose theological opinions were very similar to the later views of the Reformation Protestants, whose ranks they eventually joined.

Catharism, in the age of such nonsense as *The Da Vinci Code* and the books (and TV series) from which it gained its inspiration, has had a huge press. The attention paid to so obscure a heresy—similar to that practiced by the Bogomils over in the Balkans—has, I would contend, been rather overblown. Nor should Catharism, *pace* Dan Brown, be seen in a very sympathetic light. The *perfecti*, the elite inner leadership of the Cathars, would never have approved something so physical as a marriage between Jesus and Mary Magdalene. They were ultraascetics, despising the body and all its works, beings who insisted on living on an altogether higher plane than base humanity, even though they did admit weaker mortals—for whom love, marriage, food, and other good things of life, were permitted— if they became *credentes* (believers), in the ultimate truths. Catharism was, in a way, a dualistic religion, between goodness and evil, and a faith that owed much to the state religion, pre-Islamic Persian Zoroastrianism.

But, alas, it is also probably true that, as in the time of the Reformation some three hundred years later, there was an enormous amount of corruption and nepotism in the Catholic Church that did its reputation no good among the genuinely spiritually sensitive and seeking. Thankfully for medieval Christianity, great and wholly convincing saints come from time to time, breathing in fresh air and heartfelt renewal—Saint Francis of Assisi being the outstanding example of medieval days and, if let loose, I would add, one friar being worth tens of squadrons of cavalry to bring the spiritually lost back into the fold.

But other giants of the faith, such as Bernard of Clairvaulx, and heroic reforming popes, such as Innocent III, did not always possess the patience that those of us from a later era might wish them to have had at the time.

So, was it a good idea *to* launch the Crusades? From the Enlightenment in the eighteenth century onward, the trend has been to denigrate them. The most famous historian who has written about them in detail, Sir Steven Runciman, did not hesitate in the multivolume work he wrote in the 1950s to make abundantly clear that the Crusades should be thought of as a catastrophic mistake to all right-thinking people.

Therefore, even to pose the question that there might be a possible justification for the Crusades might seem a strange thing to be asking in the twenty-first century, as the answer would obviously seem to be no. But, surprising as it might seem, serious writers are today advocating the notion that the Crusades were a good idea, after all. These include Robert Spencer, author of *Islam Unveiled* and *The Politically Incorrect Guide to Islam (and the Crusades)* and director of the Web site Jihadwatch.org, as well as British author Daniel Johnson, in an article in *Commentary* magazine.

The leading neoconservative writer and academic Victor Davis Hanson has from time to time also written on the Crusades, from a more sympathetic angle. So, too, has the historian Thomas Madden, in his *Concise History of the Crusades* and, like Hanson, in journals such as the *National Review*. Spencer, in *Islam Unveiled* also suggests that no less than Bernard Lewis takes a similar position.

It is only natural that people should want to defend the West, especially in a time of terrorism, and the defenders of the Crusades can be put into that category. Not only that, but, as Johnson reminds us, the Crusades "took place against a background of Muslim conquest." As we saw in the last chapter, the Islamic invasions of the seventh century were what began centuries of religious warfare, and not the Crusaders. Bernard Lewis is surely right to say that, until 1683 and the second Ottoman imperial failure to capture Vienna, the armies of the Muslim powers had the military advantage, with the Christian countries on the defensive.

However, when Spencer quotes Lewis as saying that the Crusades were a response, albeit rather delayed, to the conquest of Jerusalem he is not giving the full picture of the argument that I think Lewis is making.

(Even an academic historian such as Madden has said this, suggesting that the Crusades are no different in kind from, say, an event such as the Allied liberation of Normandy in 1944. I can see the point, but Normandy came four years after the fall of France in 1940, whereas the Crusaders were capturing Jerusalem no less than 461 years after its seizure by the Islamic invaders.)

For the real point that Bernard Lewis, and other historians are making, and which Spencer omits, is that the actual truth about the Crusading period is twofold.

First, the *real* battle at the time was not so much between Muslim and Christian, but between the two kinds of Muslim, Sunni and Shiite. For example, at the time of Saladin, it was between Saladin, a faithful Sunni Muslim, and Shiite Muslim Fatimid caliphate in Cairo. Significantly, as we have seen, it was Cairo that Saladin conquered first, in 1069, becoming sultan in 1071, and only then did he go on to attack the Crusaders and seize Jerusalem in 1087, some eighteen years later. Second, Lewis, in his post-9/11 books and articles, makes an important point. The Islamic powers won the Crusades, from the thirteenth century to the twentieth, what is now the Holy Land was under just over six centuries of continuous Muslim rule.

What changed Islamic perspectives, and especially in the Arab world, was the century and more of Western incursion

into the Dar al-Islam, beginning with Napoleon's brief conquest of Egypt in 1798, France's seizure of Algeria in 1830, and
subsequent territorial losses right up to the major defeat of the
Ottoman Empire by the Western allies in 1918. Then, as David
Fromkin shows in *A Peace to End All Peace*, as does my own
Churchill's Folly: How Winston Churchill Created Modern Iraq, we in
the West carved up the Middle East for ourselves in a blatantly
imperialistic fashion. It was thus the events of the nineteenth
and the early twentieth century, and not really those of the
eleventh, that altered the way in which we all, Westerners and
Muslims alike, look at the Crusades.

This is also a point made by the historian Carole Hillenbrand in her book *The Crusades: Islamic Perspectives* and by the
medievalist Helen Nicholson in *The Crusades*. Both point out
that the first Islamic history of the Crusades, written in the
nineteenth century, was a translation of a French work, and
that the first original Muslim history did not appear until 1899.

So when Amin Maalouf writes in *The Crusades through Arab
Eyes* that the enmity between Christianity and Islam goes back
to the Crusades he is, as Nicholson points out, quite wrong. Indeed, as discussed in the last chapter, the real clash goes back
to the seventh century, when Muslim armies attacked Christian
territory.

Andrew Wheatcroft also reminds us that no such word as
crusade existed until well into the sixteenth century, when *cro-
isade* was mentioned in French. *Crusade*, as an English term, does
not predate the eighteenth century. As he points out, therefore,
none of the Crusaders, at the time, ever thought of themselves
as such—the term used by them was "to take up the cross," and
that is how the term is still translated in Arabic today.

However, as the current scholarly debate also reminds us,
twentieth-century events have completely distorted the historiography of the Crusading period, since there are plenty in the
Islamic world today who see the West as acting in Crusade
fashion to the Dar al-Islam, something that we shall look at in

more detail in the last chapter, when we examine the current
spate of Islamic terrorism against the West and the way in
which people such as Osama bin Laden manipulate the Crusades for twenty-first-century purposes.

So while I can see where Robert Spencer, Daniel Johnson,
and others are coming from, I think that, ironically, they are being as anachronistic in their view as are the current-day Muslims whose views of the Crusades they so dislike. They are all
looking at medieval events in the light of both recent history
and of what is happening in terms of terrorism and Middle
Eastern conflict in the twenty-first century.

It is important to say here that conservative academics,
such as Madden and Hanson, are surely historically correct in
saying that the Crusaders were not Western imperialists. That
is because, as the controversial historian Ephraim Karsh reminds us in *Islamic Imperialism*, it was the Muslims of that time
who wanted to build empires, not the Europeans, as he argues
was the case with Zengi, Nur al-Din, and Saladin himself.

But even there, I would add, it is not so simple. The reason
for the Islamic desire to expand was not so much economic gain
or political power—as was the motivation of nineteenth-century
Europeans—but a religious desire to conquer in the name of
the religion that they believed to be uniquely true. So to me,
even the imperialism of the eleventh century was different from
the kind we know today. If, as I think we should, we attribute
mainly spiritual motivations to the Crusaders, we ought to do
the same for the Islamic invaders, however much we might disagree with both groups today.

We need therefore to look at Crusader times in the light of
what men (and women) believed at the time, to remember that
the Middle Ages are what one popular television series calls
Strange Landscapes, in which people were very like us in many
ways but also thought radically differently from how most of us
do today. What we will discover is that the Crusaders, by their
own lights, are not guilty of much of what modern people ac-

cuse them, but that by the standards of both their Christian faith and of the teaching of the time, they were also far from innocent. In other words, they are both guilty as charged, and completely innocent, all at the same time!

One thing that defenders of the Crusades do is to give a full picture of life in the Middle East during that period. But we also need to examine how Western Europeans thought and acted, because that gives us strong clues as to why the Crusades took place at all. Any decent history of the causes makes sure that, for example, we understand what was going on in the Catholic Church, since it was a pope, Urban II, who made the call that set the Crusades in motion.

Here, I would argue, as does leading Cambridge historian Jonathan Riley-Smith, that part of Urban's motivation had nothing to do with Islam at all, but a lot to do with the internal European politics of the power of the papacy in relation to the secular rulers of Europe in the eleventh century. In particular, we need to remember the "investiture controversy," something perhaps arcane to us, but a major source of conflict between popes and princes for centuries, and which was to be a pivotal reason behind the Protestant Reformation of the sixteenth century.

This view of the Crusades, one I take myself, is now called the "pluralist" outlook, by such historiographers as Christopher Tyerman in his *The Invention of the Crusades*. (The "traditionalist" view is that the Crusades really apply to those in Palestine only — as will soon be obvious, I do not hold that opinion.) What Riley-Smith, John France, and others do is insist that all the Crusades — be they Palestinian, Albigensian, Baltic — be seen in the European historical context in which they began, and to do with the issue of papal power in particular.

In essence, the ongoing argument was over who could appoint to major ecclesiastical offices: archbishops, bishops, abbots, and similar posts in the Catholic Church. Because the Church's spiritual leaders were also major landowners, they had considerable *political* power in much of Western Europe, and, in the Holy Roman Empire, were frequently rulers of numerous small duchies and principalities as well.

Naturally, therefore, the Holy Roman emperor and other leading secular figures, such as the kings of France and of England, wanted to be able to appoint to those Church positions the men they wanted. However, being laymen, their motivation was often far from spiritual in who received what office, with the illegitimate son of a king or emperor often being appointed to a very senior church position, and at a ludicrously early age as well.

Although some medieval popes, such as the Borgias, were profoundly corrupt, many of the others were godly reformers who wanted a decent church run along properly Christian lines. Several such devout popes existed in the eleventh and twelfth centuries, and Pope Urban II and his predecessors were among them. They, too, therefore, wanted to make the leading ecclesiastical appointments, and in their case, to bestow office on spiritually minded men whose main motives would be Christian rather than political.

It goes without saying that this was a big source of conflict. In England, the dispute over investiture between the king and the pope continued until compromise was finally reached in 1107, significantly twelve years *after* Urban II had called for a Crusade.

Because it was the pope who summoned the Council at Clermont in 1095 that began the Crusades, there is a way in which it is possible to argue, as reputable medievalists make clear, that a key notion behind them has therefore nothing to do with the Middle East, or of Christians invading Islam, but of the popes finding a cause in which they, not the secular rulers, wielded the power.

As noted, many Crusades were not against Muslims at all. The Albigensian Crusade was against Cathar heretics in the south of France. Here, papal desire to exterminate heresy, and the king's desire for more power, enmeshed nicely: the pope, with the aid of the new Dominican Order of monks, was able to rid Europe of a belief that threatened the Catholic Church, and the king of France was able, through his choice of Crusade leaders, to reestablish royal control over a part of his domain that had become too politically independent for its own good.

In fact the only Crusade that could be called imperialistic, in the modern sense of that term, was also in Europe, when German knights battled in Central Europe against the pagan Poles, Lithuanians, and Livonians, and, in the process, managed to gain much extra land for themselves that, come the Reformation several centuries later, was secularized and taken over by the nascent kingdom of Prussia. There, in the territories of the Teutonic Knights, and those of the Sword Brothers, Germans did settle, and lived in large numbers right down to the middle of the twentieth century until the defeat of Nazism in World War II.

Some writers are correct in saying that we see the Crusades very much in a Protestant light. Being one myself and an author on the Reformation, I can see the danger, because such an attitude is equally anachronistic. Luther and his successors taught that Christians can have a direct relationship with God, unmediated by any human being. The Catholic doctrine, however, was that forgiveness for sins could not be mediated directly, but needed priestly intermediaries. The pope was the supreme go-between, and had the power to remit sins, and thus the divine punishment that was the inevitable result of breaking God's laws. Urban II and his successors therefore used the Crusades as a chance to remit the bad deeds of anyone who took up the cross and embarked on a Crusade, wherever that might be taking place.

This last qualification is important, for not only did those who went to the Holy Land find forgiveness, but those involved in the liberation of Spain from the Moors, German knights battling against the pagans in Lithuania, and French noblemen massacring the Cathars in the Languedoc did so alike.

Andrew Wheatcroft also demonstrates, in *Infidels*, that medieval believers had an essentially visual and nonliterary way of expressing their faith. Mass literacy is, apart from much else, a product of the Reformation. The Protestant doctrine of scripture meant that more people needed to be able to read the Bible for themselves. Our notion of Christianity as a book-centered faith is therefore more modern, and postdates the Crusades. So as Wheatcroft points out, folk in medieval times would feel they knew Jerusalem almost better than the cities nearby, and therefore anything that happened in the Holy Land would have a powerful resonance for them.

The savagery and butchery reaped against the Albigensians — all white Western Europeans — demonstrates clearly that the barbarity shown by the conquerors of Jerusalem in 1099 was not a force directed uniquely against Islam. Far from it — these were universally bloodthirsty times. Recalcitrant Saxon peasants, Cathars, Livonians, Jews — all were slaughtered indiscriminately often without any need of a Crusade, by Western knights and their soldiers throughout the Middle Ages. Certainly many innocent Muslims were massacred — and, as Spencer reminds us, Islamic armies sometimes massacred equally blameless Christians as well. Simply put, anyone who got in the way ended up dead, and not just those of Islamic faith. As most of us know by now, in time even Templars were burned wholesale at the stake by the orders of a king of France. No one was exempt from the danger of violence, and as Riley-Smith has shown, it is understandable that the Catholic Church, worried by the extremes perpetrated by those with secular power, would want to channel them away from harming the innocent at home in favor of making authorized attacks on enemies of the Christian faith.

Nowadays, the very notion of Christian holy war is abhorrent. Bernard Lewis accurately reminds us in his *Middle East* that one of the key differences between Jesus and Muhammad is that Christ was a purely spiritual leader, with a kingdom not of this world, a Prince of Peace, while Muhammad was a military and political leader, commanding troops in battle against earthly enemies, as well as being the spiritual founder of one of the world's three monotheistic faiths. Not only that, but Christian "just war" theory, from Saint Augustine onward, made it plain that a true just war had to be defensive, and that civilian casualties were expressly forbidden. Attacking the Holy Land, or Cathar heretics, was offensive, and in the Languedoc, more so than in Palestine, whole cities were massacred, women, children, and all.

The Church at the time, and their apologists since, argued that Christianity was under attack from Islam, and that the Crusades in the Holy Land were therefore entirely legitimate. (Not surprisingly, this is similar to the argument by Islamic extremists such as bin Laden that the West is attacking Islam when it either supports Israel or attacks a country such as Iraq, even if the West's reasons are resolutely secular.)

But this, too, is impossible to defend under "just war" doctrine. This mind-set insists that war can only be called by a legitimate authority. Who was such a person in the Holy Land? The West had never ruled over Palestine—it was, until the 630s, part of the Byzantine Empire. It was up to Alexius to launch a war to liberate Jerusalem, and when he asked for Western aid in 1090 and then more formally in 1095, he surely did not have in mind the actual outcome—a seizure of formerly Byzantine territory by knights from Western Europe, who kept it rather than handing it over to its former Christian owners in Constantinople. Alexius was asking the pope to help Byzantium, not to create a series of new kingdoms, principalities, and counties under Frankish rule. If Alexius had been able to launch a major attack himself, he would have been both a lawful authority and someone acting in legitimate defense, since the Seljuk Turks had invaded Byzantine territory in 1068. But none of this applied either to the pope or to the Crusaders.

Similarly, in Europe, in earlier times pagans had been won over by peaceful conversion by civilian monks, nuns and other nonaggressive lay people, who preached the Christian message in the same manner as did the early Church: slowly, carefully, and often at great human cost, without any recourse to war. Much of the Holy Roman Empire—today's Germany—had been successfully evangelized by this means, including, by monks from England, such as Saint Willibrord. Why, then, did later missionaries need the Teutonic Knights, sword in hand, to effect the same goal of conversion, and to which their own ancestors had come peacefully? Could not the Dominicans have relied upon the power of prayer and persuasion—very much as the Franciscans did, who followed the nonviolence of their founder, Saint Francis? It was not as if people in the eleventh century were unaware of the nonmilitary alternatives, being that those had been used, and very effectively, in recent memory.

However, although Martin Luther, the founder of Protestantism, rejected the Crusades as wrong; and post-Reformation Christians, twenty-first-century secularists, post-Enlightenment Westerners (as had in all likelihood, many devout seventh- and eighth-century Catholic missionaries) all united in abhorring the Crusades and their intrinsically un-Christian nature, the fact is that many eleventh-century Christians believed in the need for Crusades, and in the way in which they happened.

In other words, as Jonathan Riley-Smith's helpful books on the Crusades demonstrate clearly, the motivation of the Christians at the time was sincere, genuine, and profoundly religious, even though that might seem completely incomprehensible to us today. If we consider their perspective, we can at least understand why the Crusaders did what they did—they acted not for modern motives, but for religious ones, not to gain *new* territory, but to reclaim land lost to the major threat to the

Christian West, the forces of Islam—a specter that haunted Europe until the tide finally began to turn, centuries later, in Vienna in 1683, and in the slow liberation of the Balkans from then until 1913, a date not too far away from our own time.

This is not to excuse the Crusades—far from it! The Crusaders did not understand the basic tenets of their own faith, Christianity, for whom such resorts to armed force and military might in defense of the Gospel are wholly alien. Christ refused to wield the very sword that the Crusaders embraced so eagerly. Perhaps the great irony of the Crusades is that where they went so wrong was in taking up the tools of their Islamic foes, and launching a Christian version of jihad, a holy war, in this case a holy war against the religious group that had invented it, Islam. For the uncomfortable truth, in our post-9/11 age, in our politically correct twenty-first century, is that if the Crusades were wrong—which I would say, like Luther, they certainly were—then so, too, were all the centuries of Islamic conquest, starting in 632 and continuing, as we shall now see, against new enemies, in the Balkans and elsewhere. Holy war is wrong, whether waged by Crusaders or Ottomans, whether in the eighth century against Spain or in the eleventh against Palestine. If we agree with today's Muslims that the Crusades were indeed a terrible mistake, we must then go on to ask them to atone for their own sins in this area, as some moderate Muslims are now realizing should be done. But we can only do this if we ourselves understand what the Crusades were really all about, and why we should both comprehend their motives and at the same time condemn their folly.

THE ISLAMIC SUPERPOWER
The Rise and Fall of the Ottoman Empire,
1354–1922

THE SLOW DECLINE and eventual fall of what led, directly or indirectly, to:

- The First World War—and therefore indirectly to the Second World War
- The creation of Iraq—and thus to all the twenty-first-century chaos there
- The creation of the Jewish homeland in Palestine—and thus to that of Israel and the ongoing Palestinian dispute
- The creation of Yugoslavia, and thus the massacres and slaughter of that country's break up in the 1990s
- The humiliation of the Muslim Arab world, and thus, in recent years, to al Qaeda, 9/11, and the war on terrorism?

The answer to all these questions is the same: the *Ottoman Empire*.

Strictly speaking, the First World War was also connected to Slavic wishes for independence and the decline of the Austro-Hungarian Empire—and it was the fall of the latter in 1918 that led very directly to the vacuum in Central Europe that caused the Second World War. But had the Ottoman Empire not been in decline for well over a century, losing by 1913 most of the Balkan side of its once vast possessions, there would not have been the Austro-Hungarian seizure of Bosnia-Herzegovina in 1878, and that province's formal annexation in 1908—and thus no First World War, which began in 1914 in the Bosnian capital of Sarajevo with the assassination of the Archduke Franz Ferdinand, heir to the Austro-Hungarian throne. So I think my overall analysis is still quite safe!

There is a tendency among Western Europeans to think that the end of religious warfare against Islam ended with the Crusades. Those living in eastern and southeast Europe will swiftly disabuse one of such a mistake. For them, the five centuries and more of the suffering of their ancestors was only just beginning, from the first Ottoman incursion into the Balkans in 1354, all the way down to the final liberation of that peninsula from alien rule in 1913, no less than 559 years later.

To simplify things geographically in this book, I am going to look at the Ottoman Empire in two ways: first here, in an overview, and then in "The Poetry of Genocide," a separate chapter on later Balkan history, from the eighteenth century onward, since the fighting there, while linked to the bigger Ottoman picture, had ramifications in the former Yugoslavia in the 1990s that should, for the sake of simplicity, be handled apart from the other present-day result of the Ottoman Empire—Israel, Palestine, and the current war on terror. Inevitably there will be a small measure of overlap, but I think that to have two chapters with differing themes is an easier way to approach the topic than a straight chronology, which could get confusing and overlong.

We saw, in the sad history of the Crusades, that one of the key battles of history was that of Manzikert in 1071, when a Byzantine army was routed by the forces of the Seljuk Turkish leader, Alp Arslan, thereby dealing the Byzantine Empire a blow from which it arguably never recovered, as well as creating the power vacuum in the Middle East that made the Crusades possible.

The Seljuk Turkish Empire broke up into smaller pieces, and by the start of the fourteenth century the Anatolian Peninsula was filled with a host of tiny Turkish principalities, all competing both with each other for supremacy, and also against the rump remains of the now fatally weakened Byzantine Empire, which had also never really recovered from its temporary abolition at the hands of the treacherous Fourth Crusaders and their creation of the Latin Empire. Equally there was, after the fall of Baghdad in 1258 to the Mongols, no real overarching Islamic power either—the Mamluk rulers of Egypt were strong, but did not even begin to rule over an area as extensive as was once under Abbasid and then Seljuk domination.

The small states in Anatolia were often called *ghazi* countries—frontier lands, filled with eager warriors, or *ghazis*, anxious to carry on the fight of Islam against that faith's remaining enemies. Among these, one was to stand out and recreate an Islamic empire, one that was to last down to the twentieth century, and whose destruction in World War I has massive consequences for us even now. This was the state created by a Turkish leader called Osman (1258–1326), whose descendants, the Ottomans, were to be sultans, and, after 1517, also caliphs, even though they were Turks not Arabs, and enjoyed no descent from the Prophet Muhammad.

The Ottomans can be divided into two phases: when they and their sultans were inexorably on the rise, from roughly Osman to his descendant, Süley man (literally Solomon, in Turkish) the Magnificent, who died in 1566. Thereafter, although the empire itself continued to flourish, there were, as Jason Goodwin (of the invaluable *Lords of the Horizons*) and others argue, there was still a powerful Ottoman Empire, but no real outstanding sultan of particular ability or merit, and certainly no one of the calibre of the early members of the dynasty.

This is a history of religious warfare, not a direct history of the Ottoman Empire, so we can leave out many of the details—

books by Bernard Lewis (especially his *Middle East*), Arthur Goldschmidt (including the now-eighth edition of his *A Concise History of the Middle East*), and my own more modest *A Brief History of the Middle East*—all give precise histories over the long term of the mighty empire, one which was, as these and far more writers would attest, one of the greatest and most successful empires of all times, lasting from the fourteenth century right through until the twentieth.

As Jason Goodwin reminds us, the "Ottoman Empire lived for war." Unlike the European countries that they were to conquer, the Ottomans had standing armies, most of whose members were in fact kidnapped children from Christian families who were converted to Islam and obliged to fight for life for their new masters, the sultans. (The cavalry force, the spahis, were different—they were Turks and were paid for by land grants, or *timars*, that ended up as hereditary possessions.) These conscripts were called janissaries, and for the first few centuries were not able to marry, to ensure their complete loyalty to the sultan and his family.

In Europe, by contrast, no permanent or standing armies existed for a long while to come, and the king or ruler often depended on local feudal magnates, who could not always be coerced, to give him any army against the nation's enemies at all. Such feudal hosts were thus difficult to control, and in some of the key battles, such as Nicopolis in 1396, Kosovo in 1389, Varna in 1444, and Mohács in 1526, it was easy for the disciplined Ottoman armies to win over feudal or mercenary European forces, where discipline was shaky at best, and the aristocratic cavalry tended to have a usually disastrous mind of its own.

When the Ottomans began, as a small *ghazi* nation, there was still a small amount of the Anatolian Peninsula still left in Christian, or Byzantine, hands. Slowly but surely, however, even that became more tenuous when Turkish soldiers from the different frontier states edged forward as they squeezed the

Byzantines out. In 1326, the Ottomans were able to seize the town of Bursa, which then, for a brief period, became their capital city.

By this date, the Byzantines were as busy fighting among themselves for control of the rump of their empire as with waging war with their external enemies. Not only that, but some of the stronger Christian nations in the Balkans were also dreaming of empires of their own, and, in the case of Serb leader Stephan Dushan, of conquering Constantinople itself. (We shall look at the Serbs, and their close ethnic kin, the Montenegrins, in a special later chapter of their own.)

Dushan (1307–55), after conquering most of the Balkans, had himself crowned as emperor of the Serbs and Greeks in 1346—his empire stretched right down into modern Greece, and had he lived longer he might well have invaded Constantinople itself. As it was, he interfered in the internal affairs of the Byzantine Empire. This led one of the claimants to the then virtually moribund throne to make the fatal mistake of asking for Ottoman aid in getting rid of his pro-Serb rival. Orhan, the new Ottoman ruler, grabbed the opportunity presented by this incredible folly with both hands—in 1354, Turkish troops crossed the Dardanelles and landed in Europe, creating not only an empire there that lasted until 1922, but also a Turkish presence in mainland Europe that exists to this day.

Thereafter, it was uphill for the Turks and the opposite for the increasingly fractured powers of the Balkans. The spirit of jihad, of holy war, was powerful among all the early Ottomans, and they were some of the most successful Islamic warriors of all time.

In 1361, the Ottomans captured the town of Adrianople, on the European side of the Bosporus, and ten years later the once-strong Bulgarian Empire—the Bulgarians themselves having once come from the same area of Asia as the Turks, but who had long since integrated with the Slavic population and converted to Christianity—was itself vanquished: one group of early conquerors was now invaded and taken over by a later and more powerful horde.

By the 1380s, the once-powerful Serb empire of Dushan had imploded and splintered. The remnant of it, under Prince Lazar, was not even a pale shadow of what had gone before, and in 1389, at the Battle of Kosovo Polje (the Field of Black-birds), Lazar was defeated and killed, the only consolation being that the Ottoman leader also died, being murdered shortly after winning the battle.

The Ottomans seemed poised to venture further into European territory. Then they were stopped by a seemingly far more brutal, overwhelming force—that of Timur Leng known to most in history as Tamerlane.

Tamerlane, who reigned from 1369–1405, is now revered throughout Central Asia as their last great large-scale conqueror, someone who conquered and tyrannized millions of people. At one stage his vast empire stretched from Egypt through to northern India. Cities such as Samarkand are monuments to his egomania. While he was partly ethnically Turkish, Tamerlane was mainly of Mongol descent, and can be regarded as the last wave of the barbaric Mongol invasions in which countless numbers were butchered en masse, with whole cities annihilated, and terror spread for thousands of miles around. The only difference between him and the original Mongols was that he was already a Muslim, whereas the Il-Khans of Persia and the Khans of the Golden Horde had taken a few generations to convert. As a result, the wars between Tamerlane and his Ottoman adversaries were intra-Islamic, one Muslim army fighting another, and so do not count for our purposes as religious wars. This was lust for conquest and domination, pure and simple.

Tamerlane died en route to trying to conquer China, which was just as well for the Ottomans who, as historians have speculated, might have otherwise been wiped out, and never built the long-lasting empire they did in fact go on to rule. It is probably just as well for Europe also, since while the Ottomans were imperialists, empire builders, and conquerors, they did not possess the sheer evil and barbarity of Tamerlane, whose brutality and desire for carnage was not, arguably, seen again until Hitler in the twentieth century, over five hundred years later. In other words, the Ottomans were bad—imperialism is wrong—but they were not *that* bad.

Fortunately therefore, the Ottomans survived, even if narrowly, against the tornado from their east. Later rulers of their eastern borders were to prove a major problem for them, but never again on the scale of the Timurid dynasty—a less violent offshoot of which, the Mogols, went on to conquer most of India and to create such architectural gems as the Taj Mahal, and to last, with diminishing power, until the nineteenth century.

Strictly speaking, wars between the Ottomans and their Persian neighbors are also wars within the family of Islam—while today's frontier between Iraq and Iran dates back centuries, there was continuous war, over hundreds of years, between the Ottomans on the one side and various Persian dynasties on the other, the best known and most successful of which were the Safavids, from 1501 to 1536, and which reached its apogee under the great Shah Abbas I, who reigned from 1587 to 1629.

However, under the Safavids, Persia (Iran today) also officially converted to the Shiite version of Islam. This was to make an enormous difference. So far as the Ottomans were concerned, they were the guardians of true Islam, as opposed to the Shiite heretics in Persia. If anything, heresy was worse than simply being an infidel—the non-Muslims were ignorant of the truth altogether, but heretics were professing Muslims who should know better, and were thus regarded by the Sunni Muslim Ottomans as more horrendous than unbelievers. The Ottomans were the bastion of Sunni orthodoxy up until the abolition of the Caliphate in 1924. Furthermore, the official Ottoman version of Sunni Islam—there were four equally revered Schools of Islamic jurisprudence, all dating from before the tenth century—was the Hanafi, one still practiced in that part of the Muslim world, and regarded by commentators within and without Islam as being the most relaxed and least draconian of the four possible interpretations of Muslim law.

Having survived Tamerlane, the Ottoman armies were now able to go on to conquer the biggest prize of all: Constantinople itself, Byzantium, the heart of Orthodox Christianity and the capital of the Eastern Roman Empire for more than eleven hundred years, since its foundation in the fourth century by Constantine himself.

The Ottomans had already dispatched a European army at the Battle of Varna in 1444, a very last-minute and extremely tardy effort by the king of Hungary to slow or prevent the Islamic advance into the Christian Balkans. Now Mehmet II, known as Mehmet the Conqueror, who had ascended the Ottoman throne in 1451, decided he would do what Muslim armies had been trying unsuccessfully to accomplish for over eight hundred years, and capture Constantinople itself.

The siege has become legendary, and books continue to be written about the details, so we need not go into them here. But suffice it to say that the powerful ancient walls, and the numerous Genoese troops who had come to the Byzantine emperor's rescue, proved to be worthless against the sheer scale of the Ottoman assault. In 1453, Mehmet succeeded where all had failed. After three days of looting and pillaging, he entered the city, made it his new capital, and proclaimed himself to be the sultan of Rum—in effect, a Muslim Roman emperor. The last bastion of Eastern Christianity had fallen, and, in no small way, due to the folly and greed of the Western Christian Fourth Crusade in 1204, that had weakened the once mighty Byzantines fatally, and, from 1453, wiped them out. It is not surprising that when Pope John Paul II visited Greece, he had felt it necessary to apologize for the stupidity of the Crusades, since, in the end, it was Christian Byzantium that was their real victim, rather than Islamic rule over the Holy Places.

The Ottomans, it should be said, were more merciful to Jews than the Christians had been—Salonica (now Thessaloniki), one of the biggest cities in their empire, became for five centuries the place of refuge of thousands of Jews from Spain, the Ladino Jews, who managed to survive happily under Ottoman rule only to be wiped out in the Holocaust in the twentieth century. UN secretary-general (and later Austrian president) Kurt Waldheim was one of the key people involved during the Second World War in ensuring their transport to the gas chambers.

Christians under Ottoman rule were able to continue worshipping freely, but severe restraints were placed upon their progress. They had to pay more tax, and many public offices were barred to them. Nonetheless, under the *millet* system, under which all Ottoman subjects were placed, Orthodox Christians could continue to practice their faith, so long as they did not try to convert Muslims back to Christianity. (Thousands of Catholic and Orthodox Christians under Ottoman rule did convert to Islam, with the hideous nineteenth- and twentieth-century results gone into greater detail in chapter 5.)

The patriarch of Constantinople, having been, for all intents and purposes, more an administrator and civil servant under the Byzantine emperors, effectively continued his role under the Ottomans, since he was regarded as the legal head of the Orthodox subjects of the sultans. Other groups had similar *millets*, such as Catholics, Armenians, and Jews.

The Ottomans were repressive, and they were Muslim conquerors of Christian lands. But they were certainly not racist. What mattered was being a devout Muslim—your race, or ethnic background, was of complete irrelevance. As a result, if, say, a European converted to Islam, all offices, however exalted, were open to him, and many a Grand Vizier, the number two position in the empire, were of European origin.

In fact, controversially, so too were many of the elite soldiers and civil servants. This was the *devɔhime* system, in which boys of young age were kidnapped from their families in Christian parts of the empire, converted to Islam, and forced to live in the capital, administering the empire or forming the Sultan's elite bodyguard, the corps of janissaries. This system, it should be said, lasted only three centuries or so, not the whole length of the empire. But it was barbaric, and had devastating consequences come the independence in the nineteenth century of those regions from which the poor boys had come.

Most of the Christian subjects of the empire survived peacefully, however. Soon, even more Christians were to come under Ottoman rule. In 1517, the forces of Selim the Grim took Egypt, defeating the Mamluks. This was important for the sultans. We saw that the Abbasid caliphate had been wiped out by the Mongols in 1258. A theoretical caliphate still existed in Cairo, of Abbasid descent, but a powerless one since the real rulers were the Mamluks. Now in 1517, with the conquest of Egypt, and its dependent territories, such as Syria, the Ottoman sultans now also became the caliphs, despite their lack of Arab blood and descent of any kind from Muhammad or his family. This gave them enormous Islamic legitimacy, since the Ottoman holders of the caliphate wielded real power. The same year saw their conquest of the two holiest places in Islam, Mecca and Medina, and this gave them greater spiritual power as well.

(The local rulers of these two cities were still descendants from the Prophet, and lived there until the Saudis expelled them in 1924—the kings of Jordan today are their descendants. But the sharifs of Mecca had to be approved and appointed by the sultan, with whom the real power lay.)

Many Egyptians were still Christian, or Copts, as they are

still known. If they amounted to at least 20 percent of the population as late as the twentieth century, they may have been even more numerous back then. We forget how many parts of the Middle East have never ceased to be Christian, despite well over a millennium of Islamic rule.

Still more Christians came under Ottoman domination in 1526. These were Catholics, mostly Hungarian and Croatian, and, as the Reformation spread eastward, increasingly Protestants as well. In that year, a large Christian, mainly Hungarian army, under King Lajos (or Louis) of Hungary and Poland was routed at the Battle of Mohács. By this time, one of the greatest of all the Ottomans, Süleyman the Magnificent, was sultan, having ascended the throne in 1520.

A small rump of Hungary, including much of what is today Slovakia, managed to survive Mohács, and passed under Hapsburg rule, until 1918. But most of the kingdom, including the now gruesomely legendary part, the principality of Transylvania, was under Muslim rule, and would be until liberated in the late 1690s.

In Hungary, the Ottomans were more careful than in the Balkans proper. They did not introduce the *dervshime* system—no Catholic boys were kidnapped—and they strongly supported Protestantism, thereby winning many Calvinist Hungarians to their side. The Hapsburgs were zealous Catholics, and persecuted Protestants wherever they found them. The Ottomans realized this, and so naturally gave special rights to their Protestant subjects in Hungary, who obviously preferred not being persecuted under Muslim rule than being ruthlessly suppressed by their notionally fellow Christian Europeans, the Catholic Hapsburgs.

(Not all writers would agree with the rosy picture I have just painted, especially the writer Ba't Ye'or, whose *The Decline of Eastern Christianity under Islam* and her more controversial recent work *Eurabia* on Islam in Western Europe, both paint a far more gloomy picture of what it was like to be a Christian under

Islamic law. She may well be right in the discouraging effects that Islamic rule had in places such as modern Iraq and Egypt, in both of which areas Christianity, once so vibrant, declined very severely, and, with Islamic militancy growing worse in the twenty-first century, might soon become extinct in some parts of the Middle East altogether. But Christianity did survive in the Balkans, with comparatively far fewer converts to Islam, and there I think her portrayal of the *dhimmi*, or Christians and Jews under Ottoman rule, really is too gloomy.)

By 1529, an enormous Ottoman army was at the gates of Vienna itself, which was not merely the Hapsburg capital, but, because the Holy Roman Emperor Charles V was head of the Hapsburg dynasty, one of the most symbolically important cities in the whole of Europe.

Had the Ottomans succeeded, there is no telling how far they might then have gone—Jason Goodwin, in his book on the Ottomans, has them dreaming of conquering the whole of Western Europe, which, it goes without saying, would have had incalculable consequences for the rest of world history.

It was, as the Duke of Wellington famously said of the Battle of Waterloo in 1815, a close run thing. Ottoman raiding parties reached as far as Bavaria, in today's Germany. The heartlands of Catholic Christendom might have fallen. But thankfully for Western freedom the Ottoman attempt failed and Central Europe survived. However, the Ottoman threat had one major unexpected consequence. So legitimately worried were the Hapsburgs, under Charles V and his successors, by the likelihood that the Ottomans would invade again, and this time win, they were never able to muster enough troops within the Holy Roman Empire to eliminate the Protestants. From Luther's point of view, struggling for the survival of the Reformation, the Ottoman seizure of Hungary and near conquest of Austria could not have come at a better time.

Other parts of Europe were not so lucky, however. In fact, the Ottoman advance continued, with Rhodes, hitherto the headquarters of the Knights Hospitallers (or Knights of Saint John in Protestant countries and the Knights of Malta—their later headquarters, which the Ottomans were not able to capture—in Catholic ones), falling to the invaders, and also the key island of Cyprus, which had been under Venetian rule since the fifteenth century (and which is at the heart of Shakespeare's play *Othello*).

In addition, Süleyman was fortunate in his wars against the Persians. By 1555, what is now Iraq was in Ottoman hands, an event with twenty-first-century consequences, as it means that millions of Shiites have been under Sunni rule, and now, in our own time, want to make up for centuries of oppression, being dominated by those whose form of Islam is different from theirs.

It was not until 1571, in the reign of the Sultan known to history as Selim the Sot (Muslims are supposed to be teetotal) that the Ottomans first suffered any kind of reverse.

This was at the Battle of Lepanto, made famous because Cervantes, the author of the classic novel *Don Quixote*, was one of the sailors on the Christian side. The commander of the European ships was Don John of Austria, an illegitimate son of Emperor Charles V. Lepanto, in the eastern Mediterranean, was a major naval victory for the West, albeit too late to rescue Cyprus from Ottoman conquest. (Spain, under the notorious King Philip II, could not decide whether or not he wished to help the Venetians, who were major economic rivals of the Spaniards.)

However, as the *New Cambridge Modern History* also reminds us, Lepanto was in reality a hollow victory, since the West did nothing at all to follow it up. Further parts of the Eastern Mediterranean, including Crete, were to fall to the Ottomans, and within just a few years of their defeat, the Ottoman fleet was reconstructed and able to prevent further Western/Christian incursions into their territory.

Not only that but, in 1574, the Ottoman armies were successfully able to recapture Tunis from the Spanish branch of the Hapsburgs (who also ruled over the kingdom of Naples, now southern Italy and Sicily). From 1492 onward, there was always the faint dream among the Spaniards—and among many Catholics generally—that after the liberation of Spain from alien Moorish domination, that North Africa would also be restored to Christian rule. We should not forget that the great early Christian Church father Saint Augustine was a Berber, and that what is now Tunisia and Egypt were at the heart of early Christianity. Charles V had made a small initial conquest in the 1530s, and hopes were raised, but the Ottoman victory put paid to all such aspirations. North Africa would continue firmly under Ottoman rule and the Dar al-Islam, until the European conquests of the nineteenth and twentieth centuries.

On their eastern borders the Ottomans were also very successful, making major gains in the 1580s against the Persians, with a victorious treaty in 1590. Some historians contend that the Ottoman Empire was sliding downhill after the death of Süleyman the Magnificent in 1566, but, as we have just seen, several victories took place after that, and continued to do so right through to the seventeenth century. To me at least, even if the magnificence of Süleyman's reign was not matched by his immediate successors, Selim the Sot included, one could not say that the empire was declining at a time when its borders were on the increase. Having said that, it is hard to disagree with Arthur Goldschmidt in his *A Concise History of the Middle East* when he writes that sultans after 1566 were no match for the first ten.

From 1593 to 1606, war raged in the Balkans between the Hapsburgs on the one side and the Ottomans on the other.

(Traditionally the French had supported the Ottomans, on the basis that my enemy's enemy is my friend. Now, in this war, and for some years previously, the English were supplying them with material for weapons, including metal from bells that had once been rung in Catholic churches, which, now that Britain was Protestant, were no longer needed.)

This border war ebbed and flowed, with one side gaining the advantage and then the other. What helped to end it, and to ensure that the Ottomans did not lose, even if they could not be said to have emerged victorious either, was the religious fanaticism of the Hapsburgs, who were now, according to their own reckoning, kings of Hungary as well as rulers of Austria and Holy Roman Emperors. The Protestant princes of Transylvania dithered on whom to support—someone who was Christian, but Catholic and a believer in absolute monarchy, or an Ottoman sultan, who was a Muslim, a Turk, but allowed Protestant Christians complete freedom of worship and allowed considerable autonomy to their Transylvanian and Hungarian vassals.

In the end, the princes opted for religious freedom and political autonomy, and supported their Ottoman overlords. In 1606, at an island in the Danube usually now transliterated as Sitvatorok, the Hapsburgs and Ottomans agreed upon a draw to end the war (and with small territorial gains for the latter). A contemporary Venetian had described the thirteen years of warfare as the "slaughterhouse of men," and it was, by all accounts, a brutal time. What finally ended it, though, was not the decision of the Transylvanian princes but the fact that, from 1603, the Ottomans were also facing a major campaign on their eastern border, against a resurgent Safavid Empire, under their greatest leader Shah Abbas I. Most of Ottoman gains in the 1580s and 1590s had to be abandoned, although in due time the Persians were to lose them, especially after the fall of the Safavids after 1736.

Bernard Lewis and other writers have given much prominence to the Treaty of Sitvatorok, even though it would be best to argue that the war itself was a draw. This is because, for the first time, an Ottoman sultan granted full recognition as a monarchical equal to a Western ruler, in this case the Holy Roman Emperor. No longer was a Christian seen as a lesser being, but as a potentate of equal power.

This being a history of religious warfare rather than one of the Middle East, we need not worry about the attempts of various eighteenth-century Ottoman sultans to reform their empire and make it a more governable place. Suffice it to say here that, by the 1680s, much reform had been undertaken, and the Koprulu grand viziers had achieved much in terms of cleansing the stables. By 1682, the Ottoman armies were again on the move, this time determined to capture Vienna and eliminate the Hapsburgs once and for all.

However, they were up against a far more formidable foe than before. The Hapsburgs had created what was called the military frontier. Ethnically, this was originally a Croatian area, but the Hapsburgs settled it with whoever was best equipped to protect their domains against another Ottoman invasion. Many of the frontier warriors were therefore ethnic Serbs — and thus also religiously Orthodox — something that would go on to have enormous consequences in the form of the savage Balkan wars of the 1990s. So when the Ottomans came, the military frontier ("Krajina" in Serbian, very similar in etymology to "Ukraine," which in its day was also a frontier against Muslim Tatar invaders) was ready.

But by 1683, the Turkish armies had reached Vienna itself. The emperor fled in terror, and Prince Starhemberg, the Austrian commander, prepared for a siege. For a while, all seemed lost: Central Europe would fall to the Ottomans after all.

(The Austrian love of coffee and the eating of croissants — croissant is the French word for "crescent," the Ottoman/Islamic symbol — all date from this siege: such is the way in which small things can come unexpectedly out of major events.)

All looked lost until a Polish army under the command of their king, Jan (or John) Sobieski, came to the rescue. The Ottomans were defeated, and the siege was lifted. Once again,

Catholic Europe—and possibly all of Europe itself—had been saved from an Islamic invasion.

Soon the Austrians were to benefit from one of the greatest military commanders of all time, Prince Eugene of Savoy, the contemporary of (and sometimes co-commander with) the famous British general, John Churchill, Duke of Marlborough, the ancestor of Sir Winston Churchill and of Princess Diana (and thus Prince William and future British monarchs). Eugene was from what is now Italy, but at the time was a prince from a junior branch of the Savoyard ruling family. In a series of outstanding campaigns between 1683 and 1699, he was able to roll back the Ottomans, and to liberate Hungary from Muslim rule. The Treaty of Carlowitz in 1699 was the first major Ottoman defeat, recognizing the large scale of their territorial losses to the Hapsburg forces. It was, by any reckoning, a major disaster, from which, historians have argued, the Ottoman Empire never recovered.

This is certainly the thesis of the most famous historian to deal with this issue, the British-born, religiously Jewish Bernard Lewis, who has spent much of his academic career at Princeton University. Normally an historian's background should not matter—how important is it, for instance, that I have a Scottish-Irish father, a Welsh mother, a Virginian wife (with a small dash of Choctaw blood), and attend a Church of England congregation in Cambridge, and a Baptist one in Richmond, Virginia? However, what I have just mentioned about Lewis and his views on the decline of the Ottoman Empire are profoundly relevant to some people, and I think it is worth a small detour from our chronology since the debate his writings have engendered have gone way beyond university faculties and into the public domain.

THE DECLINING OTTOMANS AND OTHER ISSUES

There is a major problem among some writers, critics, and columnists, with anyone who agrees substantially with the thesis I have just outlined, precisely because Bernard Lewis supports it. He has in recent years become an historian who is regularly denounced with zeal by the politically correct, not least by one of the heroes of the liberal left, the late Edward Said. There is no reason why these issues should be linked—an analysis of twenty-first-century policy and a consideration of the seventeenth-century past—but alas, such is the case. So while I try to avoid historiography—the study of how history is studied, as opposed to what actually happened, it is necessary to do so here, since the issue of the decline of Ottoman civilization has become highly controversial for reasons that in reality have nothing whatsoever to do with the actual events themselves, but everything to do with where one stands on contentious issues today, and on America's often acrimonious culture wars in general. Those for whom this is tedious are recommended to skip this and proceed to the next chapter, and those for whom such debates are all important please read carefully what follows here, since I am a firm believer that these issues are sadly muddled and should, in the best interests of understanding our past, be firmly separated!

THE ORIENTALISM DEBATE:
WAS ANYONE DECLINING AND WHY?

If King George III or Benedict Arnold, during America's struggle for independence, had said that two plus two equals four, would that mean that generations of patriotic Americans thereafter would have to maintain that in fact two added to two was in fact five, since the enemies of the infant republic's freedom had decreed that the two figures combined came to four? The answer is obviously no! Two plus two equals four, regardless of the affiliation or otherwise of whoever proclaims it.

I cannot help feeling that the same applies to the issue of the fall of the Ottoman Empire, and the grievous effects today of that empire's slow decline and eventual extinction. Even if, for sake of argument, one does agree with Said over the *present-day* Palestinian issue, or with President Bush's countless critics over the desirability of the Iraq war and its potentially calamitous outcome, that does not mean rejecting what happened in the past because the proponent of the post-1683 decline of Ottoman power is (a) Jewish and (b) a key adviser to Vice President Dick Cheney over Iraq policy. (Cheney came from Washington to attend Lewis's ninetieth birthday party in Princeton in 2005, such is the reverence in which the professor is held by his fans.)

To me, either the Ottomans were in decline after 1683 or they were not, and to me it makes enormous sense to say so, because that is what the historical evidence seems to proclaim, regardless of whether Bernard Lewis is right over his advice to the Bush administration in 2003.

Also, it seems ludicrous to argue that because someone is wrong over X, *everything else* that he or she says must also be wrong—and vice versa of course, since if he or she is right over X, she or he could equally be completely mistaken on Y and Z. It might be easier to believe in everything that someone writes, or reject that person's works completely, but to me, at least, that seems to be intellectually lazy. I had grave reservations over the United States' going to war in 2003 (a) because we had no UN mandate to do so; (b) because we did so with far too few troops—with the resultant massive U.S. and British casualties and the decline of Iraq into civil war; (c) because it would lead to a massive escalation in anti-West terrorism—which has now taken place; and (d) because it would greatly increase the power of Iran, which has also now happened. (Many of these conclusions were part of a paper I wrote back in April 2002: the consequences were already that obvious long before the war started.)

When I had the pleasure of meeting Bernard Lewis in 2005

and discussing all these issues with him in Princeton, I could both see his case, which, in an ideal world sounded genuinely wonderful, with freedom and democracy prevailing in the Middle East, and yet at the same time feel intellectually obliged to reject it, since reality, tragically, and well-intentioned Western goals were sadly never destined to come together.

But I still support his theory of Ottoman decline and its catastrophic results, since the intellectual case he makes is both conclusive and overwhelming. To me, both Lewis and the British writer Robert Irwin (in his book on the debate) have demolished Said's case against the Orientalists, however much I might sympathize with the Israeli and Palestinian peace activists to whom I have had the honor of being introduced.

The historiography preliminaries now dispatched and dealt with, we can resume our story.

One of the most telling points Lewis makes in his books, such as *What Went Wrong?* and *The Crisis of Islam* is that the Ottoman Empire simply lost all interest in the outside world and in how to remain competitive in a rapidly changing international environment. We shall return to this theme when we look at the decline of the Ottoman Empire.

❧ 4 ❧

ONE KING, ONE LAW, ONE FAITH

WHEN A MONK at an obscure university in a backwoods part of the Holy Roman Empire — in the region now called Saxony — placed an academic discussion paper on a cathedral door back in 1517, he would never have imagined that he would change the entire course of world history, split medieval Christendom forever, and, as an indirect result, plunge Europe into just over 130 years of unbelievably bloodthirsty religious civil war.

Martin Luther, the man we regard as founding the Reformation, was that obscure monk who nailed his historic ninety-five theses to the door of the cathedral in Wittenberg, in the electorate of Saxony, a prosperous but not exactly intellectually world-class place in Early Modern Europe. He had, though he did not know it, created Protestantism, and ended the thousand-year-old monopoly of the papacy on the spiritual lives of Europe, thereby cleaving Western Christendom in two, and permanently.

He also unleashed Europe's wars of religion, Catholic fighting Protestant, that was to last down to the end of the Thirty Years' War, an intra-German-and later Europe-wide conflict that finally ended with the Treaty of Westphalia in 1648, which began what most political scientists now regard as the current international state system.

Now that we are sensitized to matters Islamic, we have all

become increasingly aware—or should have become, if we have not—of the internal differences within Islam, of the divergent views of Sunni and Shia, of the significance of the Battle of Karbala in 680 and the split in Islam that has resulted now for more than thirteen hundred years.

But we forget these days that, for well over a century, Protestant and Catholic were at literal, as opposed to merely spiritual, war, with armies rampaging across Europe. During that time, great states such as France suffered decades of civil war in which whole generations of families lived in fear of soldiers suddenly arriving in the village and killing all its inhabitants.

All that is true, but we cannot forget, in a book on religious warfare, that for a long period one group of professing Christians was attacking another, and all in the name of what variety of Christian faith they professed. Furthermore, if someone dared to be a radically different kind of Christian—say an Anabaptist—there was a strong likelihood that both Protestant and Catholic hierarchies alike would be after him or his, and that person might end up being killed in whichever part of Europe he or she sought refuge.

It is not surprising that one of the major political commentators of this era, Thomas Hobbes, wrote in his book *Leviathan* the famous lines that life is "nasty, brutish and short." Not only was this a major time of disease, but with civil war affecting civilians out of all usual proportions, especially as many armies lived off the land, one's chances of getting murdered or starving to death were exceptionally high. Life expectancy was indeed short because of the high risk of violence, and the constant fear made the whole continent brutish. Hobbes was right—he was entirely accurate in the nasty world in which he wrote and lived.

One of the issues that now became crucial in Europe, albeit in a different way from the present, was that of identity. This remains a vital theme—one of the main puzzles today is why upper-middle-class, educated young men, sometimes with families, decide to become Islamic terrorists and kill themselves and countless other people as suicide bombers. Identity in a much simpler form was slowly emerging as an issue even in the sixteenth century as, for the first time, inhabitants of Western Europe found that they actually had a choice—of what to believe, where to live, and what to do.

Today we take the possibility of many differing kinds of identity for granted. We can choose who we become in a way that would have been unthinkable in the more ordered world of previous generations, in which someone's entire life ahead was all but prescribed from birth.

We so take all this for granted that we forget what it usually entails. Let us look at some imaginary combinations, to see how it all works out in our confused, very atomized, and now highly postmodern twenty-first-century world, before reverting to the much simpler landscapes of Early Modern Europe.

(Here I am adapting a fascinating paradigm begun by Norman Davies, a British historian and expert on Eastern/Central as well as Western Europe, in his book *The Isles*, and also my own earlier adaptation of Davies in the 2002 edition of my book *Why the Nations Rage*).

Take two students—both fictitious—who attend the same history class at the University of Boatwright, in Virginia.

One of them is Ahmed, who is majoring in history. He was born and raised in Fairfax County, where large numbers of Muslim families may be found. He is therefore already a Virginian, so did not have to go out of state to attend its university.

He sees himself as a Virginian, although, to his surprise, down in Richmond, the old capital of the Confederacy, he encounters those who doubt his status, since they regard inhabitants of the suburbs of Washington, DC—which is what Fairfax is, in reality reality—as being Yankees, not genuine Southerners. Somewhere in Virginia, Ahmed has discovered, there is an invisible line south of which one's authentic Southern-ness is no longer taken for granted.

Then he goes, one spring break, to a Texas resort, where he finds, to his horror, that even Virginians are seen as Yankees— no one doubts down there that he is an authentic Virginian, but he suddenly discovers that to the Texans, Virginia is seen as so far north that even the homeland of Robert E. Lee is seen as almost Northern!

Ahmed is a Muslim, and in a place as cosmopolitan as the suburbs of Fairfax County, this is no problem. In Richmond, however, some folk look at him somewhat askance, as if—to his amazement—he might be a terrorist! But surely, Ahmed argues, he is as patriotic an American as the rest of them! His parents actually chose to leave Pakistan to come and live in the United States, the land of the free.

Not only that but, like many of Pakistani origin, Ahmed and his family are Sufis, members of one of the mystic sects of Islam founded in the Middle Ages that today completely abhors violence of any kind. When President George Bush came to the mosque that Ahmed's family attend, and proclaimed, after 9/11, that Islam is a religion of peace, Ahmed and his parents were there, nodding enthusiastically in agreement. How could anyone think that just because he was a Muslim, that somehow made him a suspect American, a terrorist—the kind of Muslim he so despises as doing harm to the reputation in the West of the Islamic faith.

Also in the class is Chuck, from California. For Chuck, being at the university at all is a bit of a chore. He really wants to major in chemistry, but first he has to get his humanities requirements—such as this history course—out of the way as fast as possible before going on to specialize in his real love, the sciences.

For Chuck, sports is a passion. When not in class, or in the laboratory, Chuck is on the sports field, busy at practice. Ahmed is a straight A student, whereas for Chuck grades hover around the C average, though he is keen to not let them drop below that, since he does not want to reinforce the stereotype of the academically dim sports jock who should not be in college at all.

For Ahmed, being a Muslim is a source of comfort, consolation, and, he finds himself admitting, even pride. For Chuck, however, if he had to say what his religion is, he would have to admit it is sports and beer. His family does not go to church, nor does he. He is proud of his sporting prowess, and although he is teased about being a West Coaster by the East Coast majority on campus, he is also glad to be from California, a state that has left behind the shibboleths and hang-ups of the East. Although he is white, he has an African-American girlfriend back home, something normal where he comes but which, he notices sadly, seems a rare occurrence in the Old Dominion.

Although Ahmed finds sports boring, he does like to support his friends, so Saturdays see him away from his usual haunts in the library, shouting "Go Spiders!" as Chuck and the University of Boatwright football team compete against a visiting team from some rival university in their league.

Ahmed, unlike Chuck, does not have a girlfriend, a source of sorrow. He had spotted, one day at the Spider Bookstore on campus, a very cute South Asian–American female student, who was hanging out with Douglass, the popular cashier and unofficial campus humorist and agony aunt.

Amineh was, he discovered, also of Pakistani ancestry—good news! Like him, she is upper class—they do not have the caste system in Pakistan, as they are Muslims not Hindus, but Amineh is of good family. His mother will be delighted, he thinks. . . .

But then, one evening, Ahmed saw Amineh and her friend Emily going off to a meeting for Christian students on campus. This perturbed him but he thought that Amineh was just trying to please one of her friends. But then he discovered that Amineh's parents fled to the United States because they were persecuted back home in Pakistan—for being Christians. It transpires that Amineh is a Christian as well, and so completely beyond the bounds of possibility for a devout Muslim like Ahmed, who would only consider dating a Muslim woman. Amineh may have *looked* Muslim—she was even chastely dressed, unlike so many of the other women on campus—but then, Ahmed noticed, the Christian women like Emily dressed chastely as well.

So appearances are deceptive—remember the poor Sikh who was murdered after 9/11 through being mistaken for a Muslim. Not only that, but we have many different layers of identity. We can be several things simultaneously—Ahmed is a Muslim but a Sufi, not at all a supporter of violence; of South Asian ancestry, but also a Virginian; a university student who dislikes playing at sports, but who will happily cheer on a friend who does play; he wants to get married, but also chooses to ignore the possibility of becoming even casually involved with a fellow South Asian, because she is not of the same religious faith.

Chuck is a sports jock, definitely a Californian not a Southerner, and is happy to date someone of a different skin color because for him race is simply not an issue.

Ahmed is a hyphen-American, Chuck is not—but overseas, when Chuck and Ahmed sign up for the University of Boatwright's course in Cambridge, they are both simply Americans so far as the British students they meet are concerned.

In Britain, Ahmed, who is a patriotic American, notices to his horror that many of the Muslim he encounters are nowhere near as well integrated into British society as the American Muslims are in the United States. While he was not exactly thrilled by the invasion of Iraq—which he finds himself verbally attacked over simply because he is an American—it is not a religious issue for him, as Saddam Hussein was, in any case, a very secular Arab. But this attitude appalls the Muslims he meets in Cambridge, who feel that his sense of Islamic solidarity is lacking.

Until now, Ahmed, like many Muslim Americans, regarded

himself as devout, but never saw his faith as being in conflict with his American nationality, whatever he thinks of U.S. foreign policy. To British Muslims of his own age, it is quite different, he now observes—while not all of them support violence (to his relief: several of them are Sufis like him), they are Muslims first and British second. For them, there is a clash between their citizenship and their faith, and in all cases their religious beliefs always win.

So what is Ahmed? An American? A Muslim? Can he be both equally at the same time? Or is he a man torn between two cultural identities that inevitably conflict?

I have looked at identity in the context of two American young men at a university, but there are many other examples I could have given. For example, in Britain, rivalry between soccer clubs—the precise illustration that Norman Davies and I have given in other books—is sometimes so vicious as to be deemed tribal in nature, with loyalties going beyond normal enthusiasm for sports. If a supporter, for instance, of Manchester United is fanatical for one club, and another for Arsenal, a London team, they will not hesitate to denounce each other when their two teams are playing (in the past sometimes with real violence between fans off and on the pitch). Yet if both fans are English, they will suddenly become staunch allies during international games, both supporting the English football team against, say, France, even while as fanatically they support their respective rival teams back home.

I am an example of having multilayered identity. I am a Scottish-Irish Welshman, so entirely British and Celtic, but not one drop English, which is the predominant nation in the United Kingdom. Now that regional nationalism is on the increase, being *British* rather than, say, English or Scottish has become unusual, and so I am in a minority in being British rather than anything else. I am a graduate of both Oxford and Cambridge universities, which is again unusual as the two are historic rivals. But I am also a graduate of the University of East Anglia, a much newer university that is proud of being modern and *not* Oxford or Cambridge.

I am also happily married to Paulette, an American, a native of Virginia, who is mainly of British ancestry but also of Choctaw descent—enough so, in fact, that if this had been known when she was a child she would have been obliged to attend the local black school, even though Paulette is overwhelmingly white, because of the racist views of the segregationist county in which she was born.

I would be sorry to lose my job, which I enjoy. But I would be completely devastated if anything happened to Paulette, since being married to her is far more integral to who I am than the work I do during the day. For me, marriage wins over career, any time.

So what has all this to do with the Reformation? How is it connected to the 130 years of war that we are about to examine? The answer is: a very great deal, from kings down to their humblest subjects.

When Luther nailed his ninety-five theses to the cathedral door he was blasting apart centuries of Christendom. Up until then, everyone in Catholic Western/Central Europe was *born* into Christendom—one was a member of it from birth whether one chose to be or not. Being Christian—and in particular being a *Catholic* Christian, was part of geography.

In theory, there were also Orthodox Christians, but most of them lived in areas under Islamic rule, part of the Ottoman Empire or one of the Muslim Mongol Khanates; and, a long way from the consciousness of most Europeans, there were also Orthodox Christians in Russia shaking off the Mongol yoke, and, even farther away, mysterious black Christians in Ethiopia, about whom legends existed but not much more. To Europeans, for all intents and purposes, only Catholic Christians existed, and, in that day of very limited transportation and no news media, most people did not know personally or even know anything about anybody more than the next market away, let alone in other countries or farther away.

Since the Middle Ages—and especially the investiture controversy we saw when looking at the Crusades—there was one spiritual authority, the pope, and a political one, the Holy Roman Emperor, who ruled over what is now Germany, the Netherlands, parts of Switzerland and France, and the northern part of what we now know as Italy (a country that did not exist as such until 1859).

However, by the late fifteenth century, countries were emerging that had very strong national identities of their own. Two of these were increasingly powerful—England and France. Until the early 1400s the English kings had in reality been more French than English and had ruled over much of France. But by the time we are considering, this was no longer the case, and the English kings now spoke the same language as their subjects, while the French kings finally ruled over most of what we now call France.

Academics disagree with each other furiously on when *nationalism* began—in particular, sociologists were long fond of the notion that it did not exist until the French Revolution, in the late eighteenth century. However, today, even some sociologists—such as the distinguished London professor, Anthony Smith—have caught up with what historians have suspected for some time, namely that nationalism is a good deal older than that, and that countries such as England and France were by any definition genuine nations in the *fifteenth* century, with English and French nationalism more than possible by this period.

One of the reasons why secular sociologists regard nationalism as a later phenomenon—Anthony Smith being a notable exception—is because, in what they describe as the Early Modern period, we were all still religious. Since this means, to such experts, that we were still in a primitive pre-Enlightenment fog, religion and modernity being deemed incompatible, modern notions such as nationalism could not possibly have existed.

However, even zealous believers in modernity are now coming to understand that from an historical point of view, such notions are sheer nonsense, and owe far more to the secular worldview of their proponents than to historical evidence on what real people in the fifteenth and sixteenth centuries actually thought, wrote, and did.

For by the time that France finally managed to regain most of its territory from the English, France had, many historians have shown, a clear sense of *national* identity, and one that was also closely linked with that country's *spiritual* self-identity as well. From the thirteenth century and earlier, France regarded itself as the *eldest daughter of the Church*. Not only that, but its kings were officially called *the Most Christian Kings* —here as opposed to those of the new country, Spain, where the rulers of the united kingdoms of Castile and Aragon were the *Most Catholic Kings*, a title still theoretically used by the king of Spain today.

So to be French was to be Catholic, and not merely that but to be a part by birth of the best Christian country in the world, the eldest daughter of the Church.

However, as with many historical issues, it was not quite that simple. . . .

The French Catholic Church was very loyal to the pope, all the way over in Rome. During part of the Middle Ages the popes had all been French, and for a while, during what was named the Great Schism, there was one claimant to be pope in Rome, and another equally strong claimant in Avignon, the French-speaking city in which many of the medieval popes had lived.

(Officially speaking, the Roman popes won in retrospect, so the schismatic popes in Avignon were antipopes, who no longer count; but before that brief split, all the other Avignon popes are regarded as being full and genuine popes by everyone. Needless to say, during the Schism, the Scots supported the French "pope" in Avignon; and the English, the pope in Rome.)

The French were loyal Catholics, but they were able to make an arrangement, after the Schism, whereby clerical appointments in France would be those approved of by the French king. So the Catholic Church in France was on the one hand very much an integral part of European-wide Catholicism, loyal to the pope in Rome, but also loyal to the Gallican (Gaul = France), a national church run by Frenchmen, and at the same time loyal to the French throne. With the occasional wobble, as briefly in 1516, French kings could be devout Catholics and in charge of their own country simultaneously. This had a downside—leading clergy were more often drawn from royal supporters than from the ranks of the devout, learned or godly, and French clergy were very much seen as instruments of the state, right up to the French Revolution at the end of the eighteenth century. The scope for corruption and nepotism was also enormous. But the kind of issue that so badly severed the relationship between king and pope in, say, England, did not occur in France, as the French kings had effectively won the ecclesiastical patronage battle back in the fifteenth century.

This therefore meant that loyalty to France and loyalty to the Catholic Church were simultaneously quite possible, and were indeed expected of all patriotic French subjects of the king. Devout religious observance and French nationalism went hand in hand, and, as Adrian Hastings and other authors have pointed out, one can legitimately refer to *religious nationalism* at this time without being at all anachronistic.

So when, in the mid-sixteenth century, some French scholars, a certain John (strictly speaking Jean) Calvin included, began to read of different theological views coming from outside of France, over the border in the Holy Roman Empire, there was double trouble. Not only was Protestantism heretical, according to the teaching of the Church, but it was also unpatriotic, since France was a proud Catholic country in which all loyal subjects of the Most Christian King were members of that church.

Accounts of the Reformation used to be very partisan, depending upon whether the author was a Protestant (in which case it was the best thing ever) or Catholic (in which case it was a tragic disaster). However, there is now a theologically more neutral approach to the Reformation, one that looks at the politics of what happened, without taking sides on the spiritual issues over which Protestants and Catholics still divide. It is this approach that I will follow here, since it is, I think, the best way of understanding the background and progress of the wars of religion that so damaged Europe in this period.

Historians have also traditionally disagreed with one another in their analysis of French Protestantism, the Huguenots. To some, Huguenots were mainly hard-working artisans, skilled craftsmen, usually involved in some of the newer trades, as opposed to the older crafts, such as butchers or vintners. For other historians, since the Protestants put huge emphasis on the written word, the Huguenots were primarily drawn from the literate classes, including from those middle-class professions for which a high degree of literacy was essential. Since, at their very peak, Huguenots comprised only around 10 percent of the entire French population — just over 1.8 million of an overall 18 million — one can perhaps add, as the historian Mack Holt does in his book *The French Wars of Religion 1562–1629*, that the Huguenots could have been a mix of both, depending upon whether one examines the towns, in which one kind of Protestant lived, or the Midi region of France in general, which was the most heavily Huguenot part of the country.

Either way, Holt argues, surely correctly, French Protestantism was as a result of evangelism from outside of the country — overwhelmingly from Calvin's Geneva — and also managed to survive because of the key support of many French nobles who also converted to the new faith, notably members of the Bourbon family, close blood relatives of the French Valois kings (Marguerite of Angouleme, who married Antoine de Bourbon, was a queen in her own right, of Navarre) and/or of Admiral Gaspard II de Coligny, himself part of an aristocratic nexus with close links to the court. The latter factor is important in determining where Protestantism arose, because, as in Germany, Protestants usually needed some kind of noble, or town council support simply to survive, otherwise they would have been wiped out early on. Holt shows that the main arc of Protestantism was in the south, but also with key pockets in areas such as Normandy, where Coligny's family had estates and influence.

But whether or not the Protestants were skilled artisans or urban professionals, or both, they were never a movement that gained royal support. This was, in the end, to be crucial, and shows why, for example, Protestantism prospered in some parts of Germany/Holy Roman Empire and not others; as well as prevailed in, say, Denmark, Scotland, and England, but never took off in regions such as Spain or the Italian peninsula.

Historians do agree that the kings of France regarded their loyalty to the Catholic Church, and their title as Most Christian King, as vital to their legitimacy. Their position as king, all part of the elaborate coronation ritual in Rheims Cathedral at the start of each reign, gave enormous sacramental power to the kings that simultaneously enlarged their political power over their subjects. Kings usually made much of their anointed position, but few more so than those in France.

Consequently, as Holt and others remind us, Protestantism was thus, by definition, a threat to the king's political as well as spiritual authority, since if Catholic Christianity was untrue, so, too, was a large measure of the king's right to rule over his subjects. Protestantism was not merely heretical, it was also rebellious and subversive.

When the movement for reforming the Church from within gained momentum, the kings thus had no problem with an

Erasmus, or with the other humanist critics within Catholicism. Erasmus disliked papal abuses and corruption, but nothing he said or wrote would endanger the political position within France of the Most Christian King.

Protestantism was different, however. This is why the initial instinct of the adult Valois kings, such as King François I and King Henri II, was to persecute it. In 1548, the Parlement of Paris set up the gruesomely named *chambreardente*, literally the "burning chamber," designed to root out heresy from France. In 1551, in the Edict of Chateaubriant, Protestantism was formally banned.

By that time, Calvin had spent ten years in Geneva. His great theological masterwork, his multivolume *Institutes of the Christian Religion*, which is still read today by Christians in the Reformed theological tradition that he founded, especially by Presbyterians of many stripes, was in fact originally dedicated to the French king. We forget, because Calvin is famous for his time in Geneva, that he was actually French, and that much of his key thinking was done in France before he fled in 1534, and after that, before he even arrived in Geneva, during the time he lived in Strasbourg, then part of the empire, among many French speakers and French Protestant exiles living there.

Contrary to what some have believed, Calvin was very keen on evangelism, more so perhaps than any of the other famous Reformers of his time. In particular, he never forgot his native France, and he therefore set up an institution in Geneva—which then as now was not far from the French border—specifically with the aim of evangelizing France for the new Protestant understanding of the Christian message. From 1555 onward, a steady stream of French, Geneva-trained, Protestant missionaries arrived over the border, with the aim of converting as much of France to the new doctrines as possible.

As we saw, Holt and others estimate that by the 1560s, a good 10 percent of France had been converted, largely as a result of the missionary efforts. So, too, had the Prince of Condé,

a key member of the Bourbon family, and various other important members of the nobility.

But by this time the political position in France had changed
drastically, and very much for the worse, from all sorts of points
of view.

In 1559, King Henri III, the last normal, healthy Valois
king, was killed in a jousting accident. This was a disaster, as it
led to a regency administration, which was never a good idea in
days when a strong king was an essential part of the machinery
of stable government. His eldest son was too young to rule, and
the regency was taken over by the king's widow, the Italian
princess Catherine de Médicis (of the Florentine banking family), who now also became queen mother.

This move alienated some of the court, since, in previous re-
gencies, the post had been given to a senior male royal relative
rather than, in this case, to a foreign-born woman (a double
blow against her in those chauvinistic times). Unfortunately,
though, the nearest male relatives were the Bourbons—and they
were Protestants. This made them unacceptable, but that
very fact annoyed both them and their aristocratic factions, notably Admiral Coligny and his family.

Historians such as Holt have pointed out that previous histories of the French Wars of Religion have concentrated over
much on the bewildering array of court intrigues, assassina-
tions, attempted kidnappings, and general aristocratic mayhem
that so marks this period. Since there were between 1562 and
1598 no fewer than eight religious civil wars in France, some
more bloodthirsty and barbaric than others, it is true to say that
it is very easy to be confused as to who exactly was fighting with
whom, when, and where! In addition, at various stages during
the thirty-six on and off years of fighting, foreign princes sometimes also became involved to support the different sides; remembering which German or Spanish prince or king supported
whom can also be confusing.

However, here the new historical way of thinking helps us,

as we can ignore which battle took place when and who beat who in which of the particular civil wars that now disfigured the French countryside.

Conversion to the Protestant version of Christianity is, by its theological definition of an individual becoming born again, a personal act. But when large numbers of citizens convert, they also, again by definition, create a community: in this case some 10 percent of France. Because the converts were clustered in discrete areas of the country other than thinly spread all over it, far more than just a tenth of the population was affected in the regions where they became strong.

Historians have also pointed out what would be obvious to a statistician: if one-tenth convert, that also means that nine-tenths do not, and, for the reasons described earlier, in many parts of France full 100 percent of the population remained loyal to the Catholic faith. In areas such as Burgundy, the wine growers, for example, seem to have rejected Protestantism en masse, and in the parts of the country controlled by the powerful Guise family, the devout Catholics closely linked to the rulers of the then still-independent duchy of Lorraine, the same applied in full measure.

So while nobles—the many and changing court factions—provided what soon became the military leadership of the Catholic and Protestant groups, what we really see during this period is a clash between two *communities*, one loyal to the old religion and one to the new understanding, and it was *this* clash that really made the French Wars of Religion into the mess and carnage that they quickly became.

For, as we shall see, most of the massacres, especially those of the Massacre of Saint Bartholemew's in Paris and beyond of thousands of Protestants, which sparked the Fourth Civil War of 1572–73, were committed not by troops nor by the leadership, but by ordinary men and women slaughtering fellow citizens with whom they had probably lived cheek by jowl all their lives.

The importance of this cannot, I think, be overestimated. Civil wars are always especially brutal. Americans should not think of the American Civil War, in which northern Union troops fought with southern Confederacy soldiers. In this kind of civil war, the killing is of people raised in the same town, neighbor with neighbor, people in one village of those in the village just a few miles down the road, and also of civilians murdering civilians, not soldiers fighting each other in battle.

The same would soon prove true of the Thirty Years' War, in what is now Germany, in 1618–48, and in another series of religious conflicts in the former Yugoslavia in the 1990s, and in the same region of Europe during much of the nineteenth and twentieth centuries. The fact that the reason for such conflict is religious makes civil war worse still, as it has clearly enabled ordinary people to commit far worse atrocities against each other than might otherwise have been the case. The fact that Jesus commanded his disciples to love one another, and to love even the Samaritans, who were no friends of the Jews, seems to have been long forgotten by the perpetrators of carnage in his name, which to those of us who remain religious makes these bloodbaths all the worse.

Catherine de Médicis did not want war, and she was to spend much of the period from 1559 to 1572—with the exception of what many believe to be her complicity in the Saint Bartholemew's Massacre—doing all she could to avoid conflict. But when, in 1562, troops loyal to the powerful Catholic nobleman, the Duke of Guise, opened fire and killed a group of Protestants at the town of Vassy, her initial hopes were to prove in vain. That massacre—small scale in comparison to many of those that would follow—was to begin the First Civil War, the first of eight that were to last until 1598.

By 1570, it appeared as if the Protestants were finally gaining some kind of truce with the Catholic majority. But this, it seems, was only skin deep, since while the Huguenot leaders, such as Admiral Coligny, might now be acceptable at court, at street level, the Protestant minority was as hated as ever.

Catholic court factions, led by the powerful Guise family, who were both major French landowners and also relatives of both the then non-French dukes of Lorraine and also to the Stuart kings of Scotland (Mary, Queen of Scots's mother was a Guise), remained, however, deeply unhappy at the fact that Protestants had any freedoms at all. They were also in a permanent state of loggerheads with Catherine, who was now the effective ruler of France as queen mother, despite the fact that her sons, the degenerate last members of the once great Valois dynasty, were nominally kings and in charge of the country. Catherine did all she could to safeguard a precarious religious peace and tried also to marry first one son and then another to Queen Elizabeth of England, which, since her sons remained faithful Catholics, and were not in any case so inclined, was never a realistic prospect.

However, in 1572, she succeeded in arranging the marriage of her daughter to the military leader of the Huguenots, Henri of Navarre, who was also the head of the junior Bourbon branch of the French royal family (and the dynasty from which today's king of Spain also comes). It appeared increasingly likely that he would be the male heir to the French throne if the Valois finally became extinct.

Many of the leading nobles of France of all the different factions were in Paris in August 1572 to celebrate the marriage. This included Coligny, the great French admiral and real, effective leader of the Huguenots.

Historians differ zealously among one another as to who was exactly responsible for which set of horrors that took place over the next few days. Was it all a Guise-inspired massacre of the Huguenot leadership, or was Catherine herself involved in some of the nefarious plotting (or was it even the nominal king, Henri III)? I think a consensus is emerging that the murder of the Protestant leader, Admiral Coligny, was as a result of a plot by the Guise, and when that in turn led to a wholesale slaughter of many of the Huguenot leaders in Paris, the second event was probably inspired by Catherine and the faction immediately around her and her son the king.

No one agrees on who plotted what, but what happened next was extremely bloodthirsty and the result not of court intrigue but of popular, mass-based violence and religious rage. For no sooner had the Huguenot leaders been butchered but a virtual orgy of death, carnage, and violence now erupted in first Paris and then across France, of ordinary Protestants murdered en masse by their Catholic neighbors.

One of the key things to remember in the massacres—both in Paris itself in August 1572, and then in towns across France in August–October that year, is that they were popularly and not militarily led—ordinary townsfolk massacring people who had been their neighbors, schoolfellows, inhabitants of the same town.

The importance of all this cannot be exaggerated, since it will be a facet of all similar religious or tribal massacres in centuries to come, right down to the carnage of the twentieth century—from the Balkans (where the killing was equally on religious grounds) to the deaths in places such as Rwanda (where the differences were tribal). In all these cases, *people killed people they knew* and *civilians slaughtered other civilians*, including women and children.

This pattern is seen clearly in the massacres of 1572 in France. Here I cannot improve upon what historian Mack Holt writes about them in *The French Wars of Religion 1562–1629*.

First of all, the murders were especially violent, especially those of a neighbors-killing-their-neighbors basis. As historians seem to agree, the killings were a release of popular religious tension by ordinary citizens, rather than the court-induced murders of Huguenot nobles that had just taken place. The street murders were thus religious, not political—and as Holt argues in his book and in a journal article, one cannot simply look at these events in social, economic, or political terms, since they were, at least so far as the mob was concerned, profoundly *religious* in intention.

Earlier, after 1570, one Huguenot family had been especially singled out for gruesome treatment, and when the massacres at a citywide level began, they found themselves swiftly attacked by the Catholic mob. The Gastines and their kinsfolk the Le Merciers were butchered, and in the case of one of the latter, Agnes, says Holt, she was "immersed stark naked in the blood of her massacred mother and father, with horrible threats that, if she ever became a Huguenot, the same would happen to her."

Holt then describes two contemporary accounts of the killings in Paris. They are important, he argues, because they are ritualistic in nature, using the rituals of the Catholic Church in a perverted way to bring about the desired end of ridding Paris of Protestants. This is vital to understand in our wider context, since similar motivations and ritualistic ways of murder will continue to be used for the next four-hundred-plus years.

It is, I would argue, a form of religious cleansing, similar to the "ethnic cleansing" we will see in subsequent centuries, from Serb attempts to slaughter Slavic Muslims from the eighteenth century to the present, and, above all, albeit in a different scale and context, of the Nazis to make Europe free of Jews in the twentieth.

There is also a key element of humiliation—the enemy has not merely to be killed but humiliated in the process as well—a strong need to dehumanize the victims, to make them somehow not human, so that it is easier to kill them. We swat a fly in a way that we would never think of treating a fellow human, and so if it is necessary to the perpetrators to kill people, especially those who have been neighbors, it becomes necessary to think of other human beings as being no different from, say, a fly or a pig, so that it becomes psychologically possible for those who would not normally think of themselves as murderers to slaughter those next door.

Finally, there is the need to think of the enemy as similar to a plague or virus that has to be disposed of or eradicated for the benefit of the religious or ethnic group, and this, too, is part of the dehumanizing process. In our own times, al Qaeda employs this technique, in which bin Laden likens the presence of American troops in Saudi Arabia to a plague of locusts.

Let us, in that light, examine how ordinary French citizens could come to hate one another so much that more than 2,000 innocent civilians were slaughtered in Paris, and more than 3,000 Huguenot victims could be massacred in the provinces in the weeks thereafter.

Mathurin Lussault was killed when a mob attacked his house. His wife, Françoise, tried to escape, and but broke both her legs in the process. The mob found her at a neighbor's house. They seized her and dragged her by the hair through the streets. When they discovered the gold bracelets on her arms, they cut off her wrists. She was then impaled and dragged through the streets again.

Gruesome and vile as all this is, we cannot look with superior twenty-first-century attitudes at it, as we shall see very similar accounts of equal atrocities of one group of civilians slaughtering another in our own time, and again for religious reasons, when we look at Bosnia and its atrocities from the 1990s. Human nature is the same as it ever was and modern people are no different in these respects from their predecessors.

How does Holt explain such terrible deeds? While acknowledging social and economic factors, as one has to do, he goes on to explain what I think are the real, deep-rooted causes of such horrors:

Viewed by Catholics as threats to the social and political order, Huguenots had to be exterminated—that is, killed—

they also had to be humiliated, dishonoured and shamed as the inhuman beasts they were perceived to be.

This last point is important in terms of group identity, a theme that will be ever increasingly important as time goes by. For one of the things that we shall discover is that in what the social psychologists and anthropologists call an "unhealthy" society or culture, difference, even if tiny, is not allowed, and everyone must adhere to the religious, tribal, or in the case of sixteenth-century France and the pure Islamic or Hindu state dreamed of by modern extremists, both national and religious at the same time kind of place. France was pure Catholic, and anyone who rejected the faith of France was not only a religious traitor but a political one as well.

While there is little doubt that the king and his mother, and the wider Guise circle of hard-line Catholics around them, were, in some ways yet to be agreed upon, complicit in the massacre of the Huguenot nobility, even the king realized that wide-scale massacres of ordinary Protestants was not the way to solve the French religious problem. But this was not seen or understood by the populace, who were sure that he was behind them as they murdered increasing thousands of his Huguenot subjects.

But perhaps even more important—and this again will be a recurring theme—the mob were certain that God was on their side.

For a long time, writes Holt, leading Catholic preachers had proclaimed in pamphlets and from the pulpits that the Huguenots were "wild beasts," deserving of death. Various portents had taken place in Paris in 1571–72, in the run up to the massacre, that convinced ordinary and superstitious Parisian Catholics that the wholesale slaughter of what they saw as the Protestant plague was nothing less than the will of God.

We are going to look at the Balkan wars in more detail later, since so many of these themes recur. But let us leap ahead just

a little and look at the Carnegie Commission Report into the
wars there just before the First World War broke out in 1914.
The Carnegie Commission interviewed some Greek soldiers,
and the results are fascinating in the light of what we have just
seen in relation to the massacres of the French Wars of Religion. The Commission commented on what they heard:

> Deny that your enemies are men, and presently you will
> treat them as vermin. Only half realizing the full meaning
> of what he said, a Greek officer remarked to the writer,
> "When you have to deal with barbarians, you must behave
> like a barbarian yourself. It is the only thing they under-
> stand."

Add to this what religious conflict expert Mark Juergensmeyer calls the "cosmic dimension"—the blessing of God upon
the massacres—then the way in which one group of civilians
can kill another becomes comprehensible, albeit of course
never excusable! From France in 1572 to Greece in 1913, and,
one could add, in numerous instances of religious conflict since
then, the places may change, but the patterns of behavior remain exactly the same.

By 1584, the situation in France became truly grave. Since
the last Valois kings were not of the fathering kind, and they
had no close male relatives, the new heir to the throne was the
leading Protestant prince, King Henri of Navarre, the head of
the Bourbon branch of the ancient French royal dynasty. This
created a major crisis. The zealously pro-Catholic faction, the
Holy League, was torn, because on the one hand the sacred line
of French kings was male, and yet the male heir was a Protestant heretic. There were heirs in the female line who were
Catholics, but one of these was a Spanish infanta (princess),
and that was politically unacceptable to many in France, since
Spain had long been a national enemy. (In any case, the origi-

nal female line heirs to the throne were the English monarchs —
the Hundred Years' War between England and France had
been fought over this very issue.) So when Henri of Navarre
became King Henry IV of France, under the Salic Law rules
that allowed only male succession, the fighting between Protestants and Catholics became all the more acute.

Then in 1593 Henri transformed the situation — he converted to Roman Catholicism. Suddenly the papal objections to
him no longer applied, as he had ceased to be a heretic. Those
wanting to end thirty years of vicious civil war rallied around
him, and the hardliners of the Catholic Holy League were politically outmaneuvered.

His enemies ascribed to him the saying "Paris is worth a
mass" as the reason he gave for his conversion, and that is also
the story that has been traditionally told of why he switched religious affiliations. Some historians — Mack Holt among them —
deny he ever said anything of the kind, which in some ways is
a shame, akin to the discovery that King Alfred never burned
cakes, and other familiar tales from our childhood. But whether
his conversion to Catholicism was a genuine religious change of
heart or whether it was a cynical move to end the war and to
consolidate his own power (my own hunch), it did have the desired effect. He was now able to occupy Paris, and the eight
civil wars, spread over three decades, finally came to an end.

There had been various edicts issued under the last Valois
kings, under the regency of Catherine de Médicis, that had
granted limited rights to Protestants. But in the context of religious civil war, none of them had lasted very long, and all had
eventually proved futile.

But in 1598, when Henri IV of France, the first of the Bourbon kings, issued the Edict of Nantes that gave religious freedom to the Huguenot minority, the grant of toleration stuck.
Protestants were now integrated into French society, and allowed the religious liberty that they had craved for so long. But

it was a precarious life for the Huguenots, since what one king had granted—and a formerly Protestant one at that—a more devoutly Catholic king could, and one day did, take away.

When the edict was repealed by Henri's descendant, King Louis XIV, in 1689, it proved a financial, economic, and social disaster for France, since the Huguenots, who hastily immigrated to North America, the northern part of Ireland (like my own ancestors), the Netherlands, and the Protestant parts of the German Holy Roman Empire, were some of the most skilled workers in the country, and took all their many talents with them when they fled. The German electorate of Brandenburg (later called Prussia), Great Britain and the British colonies in the New World were all to reap considerable economic and social benefit from the sudden large influx of fleeing Protestants from France.

It was not until the coming of Napoleon, in the 1790s (and later as emperor), that in France both Protestants and Jews, the other non-Catholic grouping, were finally given lasting and permanent civil liberties, which they have to this day. Now, as we shall see, France is almost aggressively a lay, secular state, with all the potential for conflict with a new religiously different minority within its borders, the Muslims. Like the Huguenots before them, the current Muslim population in France does not hesitate to fight back and to stand up for its rights, with all kinds of implications.

In the end, the Huguenots lost out for two reasons. Firstly, they were a minority, so were permanently and literally outgunned by their majority Catholic opponents. But they also lost the crucial identity war—they were always seen as an alien intrusion into the French national consciousness, like, as we have just seen, a plague, an infection that has to be purged for the body to remain healthy. In a war of Us and Not-Us (to use modern sociological language), so long as Protestants were defined as Not-Us in a state in which, to be accepted as Us, one had to be Catholic, the Huguenots were not going to win.

It took the drastic events of the French Revolution, an event that was fanatically opposed to religion of any kind, for Protestants to be accepted as full and equal citizens of France. With France's Jews the acceptance took far longer still—in the 1890s, the venomous anti-Semitism of the Dreyfus Affair, in which a Jewish army officer was falsely accused of a crime, and which led to near civil war, Jews remained outsiders; and if one looks at the very high degree of willing collaboration in the Holocaust of French people during the Vichy period of 1940–45, it is obvious that anti-Semitism was far from dead even then. The fact that a fascist, racist candidate came second in that nation's presidential election in 2002, and the violent protests in 2005 and 2006 by the Muslim minority, at their ill treatment, shows that France's problems with assimilating religious minorities are far from over.

Over in Germany, there was warfare of a kind for well over a century, culminating in the exceptionally bloodthirsty and vicious Thirty Years' War, fought between 1618 and 1648. Similarly, in the Netherlands, the Protestant part of which especially was trying to break away from Catholic Spanish rule, the struggle for independence has sometimes been called the Eighty Years' War, with the northern half becoming the present-day Netherlands, and the southern, now once again Catholic portion, being today's Belgium. (I should say here that because of the nature of warfare in those days, fighting was not always continuous—there were times when soldiers had to go back and tend to crops, or when rulers ran out of money to pay their large mercenary armies. But the final conflict in Germany has historically always been referred to as the Thirty Years' War, and I am happy to stick to the familiar names, the war in the Netherlands also being called the Dutch Revolt.)

Here, too, religion was for most of the period the heart of the struggle. In France, the *Holy* Roman Emperor, Charles V, and his successors who used that style, took the holy part of their title as integral to their role as emperor.

Here again the issue was: what kind of country would the Germanic/Dutch part of the Holy Roman Empire be like? Would it be a Catholic country under a Catholic Holy Roman Emperor, a ruler whose position was bolstered by coronation by (or, after Charles V, official recognition by) the pope? Or would religious diversity be permissible within its borders, with Catholic states and Protestant states existing cheek by jowl? (The idea that mere ordinary citizens could make a free choice themselves was still too radical a concept in this part of Europe—*true* religious liberty in the sense that we understand it was still a long way into the future.)

Let us look first at an overview of the key issues of the war between Christians—the exact campaigns and battle details need not detain us—and then at the lessons they learned then, when it finally finished by 1648, and the still-powerful repercussions that exist for us today in the twenty-first century, especially in the religious tension between the West and the Islamic world.

When Luther made his grand gesture in 1517, all of Western and most of Central Europe was firmly under the command of Roman Catholic Christendom. In theory there were two rulers, the secular one, the Holy Roman Emperor, a title that went back to the coronation of Charlemagne in 800 by the pope, and the spiritual leader, the pope himself.

In practice, many states had long since broken away from the empire, and others, such as the countries of the British Isles, including France and Scotland, had never been part of it at all. The heartland of the empire was now what we call Germany (a country which, we should not forget, technically never existed until 1870), but it also contained what is now the Czech Republic (then called Bohemia), Austria, the Netherlands, Belgium, Luxembourg, and, notionally at least, before 1648, Switzerland, much of northern Italy, and large parts of what is now Croatia, Slovenia, western Poland, and also eastern France. Since, by a series of hereditary accidents the emperor, Charles

V (Karl V in Germany, Carlos II in Spain, so I will use the English version of his name) was also king of Spain, and ruler of much of Italy, Austria, and the Netherlands, not to mention the Spanish colonies in South America, Europe had, in Charles, the most powerful ruler at least since Charlemagne in the ninth century, if not since the days of the Roman Empire that fell in the West in 476.

But even though kingdoms such as France or England were decidedly independent of imperial rule, all of Western Europe was firmly Catholic, under the spiritual command of the pope — the same situation that we saw earlier when we considered the Crusades.

When Catholic and Orthodox Europe split in 1054, by this time Orthodox Europe was either under Muslim (Ottoman) control, or that of the czars of Russia, who from the fall of Constantinople in 1453 down to the Russian Revolution of 1917 always considered themselves as the spiritual heirs of the Byzantine Empire, with results that would become important by the nineteenth century.

But Russia—the grand duchy of Muscovy and its neighbors—was a long way away. Orthodoxy was thus not a threat, and the real danger from outside was Islam.

We must not forget that, until 1683, the Ottomans were usually militarily more powerful than any single European nation, even despite the naval battle over the Ottoman fleet at Lepanto in 1571. At the time of the Reformation, the Ottomans ruled most of Hungary, and were therefore a major military threat to Central Europe (over most of which Emperor Charles V and his brother Ferdinand were rulers) and other Islamic powers predominated in North Africa, which directly threatened Charles both as king of Spain and also as ruler of southern Italy.

So while the proper place to look at the Balkans is elsewhere, we must remain aware of the shadow that Islam created over the whole of Europe during the initial phases of the Refor-

mation—indeed there are those who argue, with some legitimacy I feel, that but for the constant background of the Islamic
threat to Europe, Charles would never have tolerated the Protestants in his midst and would have cheerfully tried to strangle
the Reformation at birth.

The fact that he was never *quite* powerful enough to do so—
although he occasionally came close in the many wars in his
reign—meant, I think, that Protestantism was able to survive in
a way that might otherwise have been impossible. For several
decades, the majority of people in what is now Austria, for example, converted to Protestantism, and it was the military might
of its Hapsburg rulers, along with the powerful missionary efforts of Catholic religious orders such as the Jesuits, that
turned the Austrians into Catholics, which faith that country
maintains today. Without the menace of Ottoman invasion
lurking forever over the horizon, the Lutherans of Germany
could well have suffered the same fate as their coreligionists in
the Hapsburg lands.

The main issue to Charles, and to the leaders, lay and ecclesiastical, of the empire, was that anyone born within Europe
was *by definition* a Catholic, a citizen of a Christendom that, despite being divided politically—England, France, the empire,
Denmark, and so on—was spiritually all under the authority of
the pope.

Thus, when Luther began the Reformation, he was being as
political in his actions as he was spiritual, disobeying not only
the decrees of the pope, but also the secular authority of the
emperor, his political overlord.

In other words, Europe was no different from many a
Muslim country today. Since 9/11, endless commentators have
reminded us—quite correctly—that there is no separation between church and state in Islam. What we forget is, that at the
time of the Reformation, *there was no such distinction in the Christian West, either.* The importance of this cannot be exaggerated.
In looking at contemporary Islam, we are looking at our own

past. The split between church and state we take so much for granted today in the West is really, in historical terms, a comparatively recent concept. (Just ask the question: could a known, avowed atheist ever be elected president of the United States? How long ago was the possibility of a Roman Catholic president regarded as a major electoral issue?)

To Charles V and many of his contemporaries, the issue was stronger still—anyone disloyal to Catholicism was a traitor in every possible sense, spiritual and political alike.

Able experts on the Reformation, such as Euan Cameron, are thus right to play up the political aspects of what took place. The empire, at this time, was not a unitary state, but an amalgam of quite large local principalities, such as Brandenburg or Saxony (from which Luther came), a series of ecclesiastical states in which, for example in the archbishoprics of Mainz and Cologne, the archbishop or abbot was the secular as well as theological authority; and myriads of tiny principalities, some just a few square miles, under barons, knights, and counts; along with several major cities, such as Frankfurt or Ulm, where the city owed direct allegiance to the emperor and thus was not under the control of any intermediary duke, archbishop, or other kind of single ruler. There were, until 1803, hundreds of these, some small, others much bigger, but in theory all owing allegiance to the common emperor.

In practice, however, the rulers of some of the larger states wanted to be able to run their own show, without outside imperial interference. This was something that Charles V wanted to stop, and which the princes and knights were determined would happen. This is crucial to the success of the Reformation, because without the support of secular dukes, electors, and knights, Luther would never have survived at all.

He would, in fact, have met the fate of an unfortunate Bohemian fifteenth-century reformer, Jan Hus, who tried something similar to Luther a century or so earlier. In 1415, Hus had to appear before the then emperor and his council at the town of Constance. Despite being promised safe passage, Hus was captured and burned to death.

Luther came within a hairbreadth of the same fate himself, at the council (or Diet, as it was officially called) at Worms, in 1521, where he was arraigned before the emperor and all the secular and ecclesiastical rulers of the empire. He is famously supposed to have refused to recant, with the words, "Here I stand, I can do no other, so help me God." Whether or not he actually used those very words, one can say that Worms is where Protestantism really began—up until then it had been more of an academic debate than serious defiance—since the gauntlet of disobedience had been thrown down in front of no less than the emperor; and from now on, what had been a spiritual discussion transformed itself into a serious political act, with secular, and soon military, consequences as well.

Cameron and others (I have written on this issue elsewhere) are surely right to say that without political intervention there would have been no Reformation. Luther was "kidnapped" at Worms, and by his own side, the forces of his political overlord, Frederick the Wise, elector of Saxony. The Diet had banned both Luther and his teachings, and without Frederick's protection—initially locking Luther up for his own safety in the fortress of the Wartburg—Luther would swiftly have been put to death, as Hus had been a century before. As it was, Luther survived, and many Protestant princes and town councils converted to the new understanding of Christianity. *Protestantism* is literally a *protest*, against the persecution of Luther and his followers, and the attempts of both pope and emperor to crush the infant movement at birth.

Writers point, correctly I feel, to the importance of the Free Imperial Cities—those outside of the principalities and other places within the empire—to choose the new faith. Admittedly, it was usually only people of property—wealthy merchants and the like who could vote—but what is interesting about these places is that here the Reformation was a popular local decision, not something forced upon the populace by the whim of a prince, duke, count, or knight. In the Free Imperial Cities, the Reformation really was a bottom-up decision rather than an imposed top-down one chosen by a single person, the ruler.

It is possible to argue that, in many parts of the empire, as in England—where Henry VIII effectively introduced the Reformation to get a divorce that the pope refused to grant—the decision to become Protestant was as much a political one as a spiritual matter. Older writers, keen to show ordinary people abjuring a corrupt Catholicism in favor of a new, dynamic Protestantism, often played this down in previous histories of the Reformation.

Certainly, at grass-roots level, among, say, peasants and artisans, and in the Free Imperial Cities, it *was* a genuine option to follow Luther. But in most of the empire, dominated by traditional, hereditary rulers, whether as powerful as the elector of Saxony, or an imperial knight ruling a mere few acres and a castle, the decision was made by one person only. Often that was as much a political decision—based frequently on an incipient sense of German nationalism against an Italian pope—as a genuine spiritual conversion made on theological grounds.

I am using the expression *nationalism* in a way that many historians would support, and many sociologists and others would strongly oppose. Historians tend to feel that you cannot understand the Reformation in a political sense unless you admit that nationalism was a strong, potent force as early as the sixteenth century. Marxists and sociologists prefer to insist that nationalism was an invention of what they term *modernity*—modern society of the kind recognizable today—and that to talk about nationalism before the French Revolution and 1789 is impossible. Historians and a few brave sociologists such as Anthony Smith of the London School of Economics and the late Adrian Hastings would beg to differ. No modern-day, unified state of Germany existed until 1870. But Germans as an ethnic group have existed for thousands of years, and the Reformation had one very significant theological/political by-product that accidentally created a much stronger sense of German self-identity than had been there before.

Luther's theological teaching can be boiled down to the rediscovery of two ancient Christian tenets: *sola fide* and *sola scriptura*. These totally overturned hundreds of years of Catholic Church teaching, and transformed the nature of Christianity permanently—globally in fact, since Protestant and Catholic Christianity are now worldwide entities with far more followers in the Two-Thirds World than in either Europe or North America.

The first one, *sola fide* (by faith alone) overthrew the right of the Catholic Church to say who was and who was not a Christian. In time, although Luther and his followers in what is called the Magisterial Reformation did not understand this, the fact that one only became a Christian through individual faith had the powerful result that led in time to the United States, freedom of church and state, and the crucial difference between the West and Islam; namely, that religion is a private free choice, and that the state and the spiritual realm must be firmly separated. Up until then, if a person were born in Christendom, he or she was a Christian, as if it were a nationality. Now the nature of Christianity was no longer just a matter of physical birth, but of spiritual awakening or rebirth—the concept Chuck Colson made popular in his famous book *Born Again*, which is in fact no more than a quotation from the first century AD foundational teachings of the Christian faith.

The second rediscovery from ancient Christianity was *sola scriptura* (literally, by scripture alone). This meant that individual Christians could interpret the Bible directly, rather than have an infallible Church impose a meaning for them. In addition, the Catholic Church had also evolved the doctrine that the historic teaching of the Church, as developed over centuries, was fully equal to that of the Bible itself. This is why, for example, Catholics believe doctrines about Mary that Protestants reject, and have faith in places such as Purgatory that Protestants do not believe exists. It is also why today there is one pope in Rome, still head of the Roman Catholic Church, but hundreds of Protestant denominations, including many in America that exist nowhere else in the world. This is how American Protestants can encompass those as far apart politically as Jim Wallis and Jerry Falwell, whereas Catholics are permanently wrestling with the latest statement from Rome that defines what they are supposed to believe.

It also meant that everyone could read the Bible in their own language, something that contributed not just to literacy — if one desired to read the Bible, one had to first learn how to read — but also, as sociologists such as Benedict Anderson, of the much-quoted book *Imagined Communities*, has pointed out, to the subsequent rise of nationalism.

While Anderson agrees fully with the idea that Germanic self-consciousness goes back to reading the Bible in the vernacular, he disagrees with the late Adrian Hastings, who, in his equally oft-cited book, *The Construction of Nationhood*, stated that it virtually helped create nationalism in Germany, such a phenomenon having already long existed in nation states such as England and France: Being German *and reading the sacred text of one's faith, the Bible, in one's own language, German*, caused a huge shift in internal German national consciousness, one that had not really existed before.

Germany continued to be a myriad of small principalities, bishoprics, counties, and other similar states, each one loyal to a local ruler and theoretically to the Holy Roman Emperor far away in Vienna. But now that there was one Bible in German, written in a single dialect — Germans still today *speak* a whole variety of Germanic dialects locally — that all Germans used for reading purposes, a sense of one's being not just a Hessian, Prussian, Bavarian, or whatever, but also a *German* now arose. This was a slow process — no single German state existed until 1870, and, except for 1938 to 1945 under Hitler, Austria, a

German-speaking state, has never united into one political en-
tity with the rest of Germany. (German-speaking Switzerland
has been separate for centuries.) But Germanic consciousness
was slowly arising, to reach a terrible and bloodthirsty crescendo in the Third Reich in the twentieth century. This eventually superseded the Protestant loyalties of the north, and the
Catholic equivalent in the south, with results that we all know.

To me, therefore, all this goes back to the Reformation, and
to one of its most unintended results, the rise of nationalism.

This is relevant to a look at the history of religious warfare
in this sense: that up to and including the Thirty Years' War —
of which much more soon — people identified themselves religiously as much as anything else. In more recent times, we have
had secularization in Europe, so that both ordinary citizens and
their political leaders have found other means of identifying
both themselves and their political unit of loyalty, which is now,
as times have changed, the nation state. Nationalism can and in
many cases has superseded religion as a focus of loyalty, and
that is why I tend to think that historians are right in saying
that in *Western* Europe, we have not had, since the end of the
Thirty Years' War in 1648, any major wars of religion.

However, in *Eastern* Europe, that was not the case — religion
was the main marker of identity imposed by the Ottoman Empire, since the split between church and state that arose in the
centuries after the Reformation in Western/Central Europe
never took place, either for the Ottomans, or for their Christian
subjects.

Long term, the effects of Protestantism were to prove
wholly beneficial for those who believe in human rights, liberty,
and, in post-Enlightenment times, those of no religious faith at
all. For as people began to realize by the eighteenth century, if
it is possible to choose your own expression of Christianity —
and by that time Protestantism was already divided into Lutherans, Anglicans, Calvinists, Baptists and many more groups
besides, some of them, in England at least, also politically very

radical—then it might be possible to choose no religion at all. The toleration of religious dissent, as African Christian and Yale professor Lamin Sanneh has demonstrated powerfully, and of the right to be an atheist, has strongly Protestant roots, and thus even the Enlightenment, to which many agnostic and nontheist liberals look back with such gratitude, is in fact a direct, albeit unplanned and unexpected, legacy of the Reformation. Without Luther's defiance of the secular and ecclesiastical authorities of his time, we would not have the freedom of religion, and liberty of conscience, that we in the West enjoy today.

In other words, and many secularists would disagree with me here, no Reformation, no Enlightenment, and thus no Modern Era. Modernity is the illegitimate child of a religious event, a notion that secularists would firmly reject, but a theory that to me makes perfect historical sense. This is important since, I would think, if we can persuade moderate, peace-loving Muslims that the West is not in fact secular in foundation, but religious—including the freedom to reject religion altogether, of course—then they are far less likely to reject Western civilization than they are at present, and more likely to side with us against those extremists in their midst who wish to bring us all crashing down and into an Islamic caliphate in which no freedom of thought is allowed.

Luther's decision to challenge the power of pope and emperor forever sundered Western Christendom in two, Catholic and Protestant. That division has never been mended, and, with Christianity now a global faith—one that has, on the Protestant side, probably thousands of diverse denominations of all different kinds and sizes—it is most unlikely ever to happen.

Initially Luther and other Reformers, such as Calvin (a Frenchman but based in Geneva), and Zwingli (who was Swiss and centered in Zurich), all believed that the rulers—or *magistrate*, to take the lowest grade, hence *magisterial*—had the right to impose true religious practice on the people. In a place such as Saxony, where Luther lived, this was the ruler, and in cities such as Geneva or Zurich, this was the democratically elected local council.

However, the pope and emperor did not want to give up what they felt was their overarching jurisdiction. The elector of Saxony or the town council of Zurich might think that they had the power to determine what their subjects believed, but to Catholic leaders, Christendom remained one and undivided.

This resulted in more than a hundred years of off-and-on warfare in Europe, in which, over the course of time, probably millions of people perished in the slaughters that followed.

It is probably unnecessary to look at the myriad small wars, alliances, and similar events that took place in Central Europe—principally in what are now Germany and the Netherlands—in the run-up to the major war that broke out in 1618. As we saw, too, Protestants owed their survival not just to nationalistically inclined counts and Imperial Free Cities, but also to the fact that the emperor, particularly Charles V at the peak of his power, was seriously overstretched financially and militarily, especially by the continued need to prevent Ottoman advances either back into Spain or from the conquered parts of Hungary into Austria and the heartlands of Europe. We know now that the sieges of Vienna in both 1529 and 1683 showed that Central Europe would in fact stay safe from invading Islamic armies, but they did not know that then; and the menace from Constantinople, and the sheer expense of keeping the Ottomans at bay, helped to keep the sometimes heavily beleaguered Protestant parts of Germany both spiritually free and politically alive.

In 1532 the Protestants were able to wrest an agreement on toleration—the Peace of Nuremburg—out of the emperor, as he had just been obliged to defend his realms against the Turks. But as the Ottomans then had to fight wars against the Persians, Charles was able to win victories not only against Islamic forces but also against the Protestant parts of his empire. However, in due time, the Protestant groupings were finally able to become sufficiently powerful to oblige the emperor to agree to a more permanent toleration settlement. This was the Peace of Augusburg of 1555. In essence, this froze the Protestant/ Catholic map of Germany—even in the twenty-first century, those parts that were Protestant then (mainly in the north) are so today, and those that were Catholic (predominantly in the south) remain so, too. The rulers (or in the case of the Imperial Free Cities, the councils) had the right to choose what version of Christianity they would follow. This was encapsulated in the key phrase *cuius regio eius religio* (which roughly translated means "whose kingdom his religion").

So for rulers, and those lucky enough to live in the Imperial Free Cities, there was religious liberty. However, it did not extend to the ordinary subjects—if someone were, for example, a Catholic living in Brandenburg or a Lutheran in Bavaria, the city's ruler still had the right at the least to persecute the person and, at the extreme, to put him or her to death. Freedom for princes did not mean equally free rights for their citizens.

Nor did the other, growing variants of Protestantism have freedom, either. No liberty was given, for example, to Calvinists, and in the course of time several Protestant rulers switched over to the Calvinist version of that faith. Nor did any of the Anabaptists have freedom, and, as Anabaptists believed, in what historians describe as the Radical Reformation, that church and state should be entirely separate, they ended up being persecuted by everybody, and in the case of Münster, a town they controlled briefly, being massacred as well. (The Mennonites in America today are the spiritual, and sometimes direct, descendant of these Anabaptist groups—Baptists are historically a slightly different branch of Protestantism, one that has mainly English origins.)

Charles V abdicated in 1556, his mission to restore the powers of Emperor Charlemagne and a united Christendom in ruins. He was succeeded as Holy Roman Emperor by his brother

Ferdinand—who did all he could to wipe out Protestantism in Austria, the lands the Hapsburgs controlled directly—and in Spain, Italy and the Netherlands to his son, Philip, who became the infamous King Philip (Felipe) II of Spain.

Philip is the person against whom the notorious "Black Legend" has been written, a tyrant who did all possible to crush dissent wherever he found it, in particular using the now legendary dark powers of the Spanish Inquisition to put Protestants in the Netherlands, and those of Jewish or Moorish ancestry to death. In England he is also well known for attempting to invade that country by sea in 1588, in the failed Armada that was both defeated militarily by the English navy and meteorologically as well by severe storms, which Queen Elizabeth I and her subjects felt was divinely sent.

However, although one cannot, as some brave historians have done, ever defend or excuse such wide-scale tyranny and oppression, it is worth remembering that there is another side of the coin.

At Oxford, my college, Balliol, was near Martyr's Memorial, the place where, in the 1550s, numerous Protestants were burned at the stake during the reign of the fanatically (and half Spanish) Queen Mary I, whose tyranny is long remembered, and who was briefly married to her cousin Philip of Spain. Balliol's vice master in the late Middle Ages was John Wyclif, an early proto-Protestant, who was lucky enough, thanks to political protection, to avoid the fate of his European contemporary Jan Hus, who died by being burned at the stake.

However, at Cambridge, my college was originally a Roman Catholic foundation (in 1896, long after toleration for Catholics had come), and to get there I pass the Church of Our Lady and the English Martyrs. These martyrs are all Catholics who were put to death in the reign of Queen Elizabeth I, the ruler who effectively established Protestantism as the permanent religion of most English people.

Finally, my wife often lectures in the British town of Bedford, from which John Bunyan, the author of the classic *Pilgrim's Progress*, comes. He was a Protestant, but of the wrong, non-Church of England, sort. He thus spent much of his life in jail.

In other words, during this period, in effect up until the 1680s, much of Europe, while religiously diverse, nonetheless had no real freedom of religion in the sense that we understand it today. Being the wrong kind of Christian could still lead to one's death, and sometimes a horribly violent one—countless thousands were burned alive at stakes, and Anabaptists, because they believed in baptism by immersion, were often killed by drowning, in a macabre and deliberately ironic method of execution.

Two things made all the difference—the first was the Thirty Years' War; and the second, the feeling in many parts of Europe after it that such carnage and economic catastrophe must never be allowed to happen again. On top of that, a new way of escape was beginning to open—the New World. Religious freedom was not always available even there, as witch trials in Massachusetts and the persecution of groups such as Baptists in Virginia were to demonstrate. But slowly things were changing.

The key thing to remember when we look at the outline of the Thirty Years' War is that *the religious is political*. We have Protestant countries fighting Catholic countries, with the ultimate aim of religious victory. What changed everything was, I would argue, the decision for purely dynastic and national reasons of the French, led for much of the conflict by no less than a Catholic cardinal, Richelieu, to side with the Protestant participants because of France's long-lasting hatred of the (equally Catholic) Hapsburg dynasty. Their assistance to the anti-imperialist forces began around 1632; and there are those who contend, I think with good cause, that this marked the end of purely *religious* war in Europe, until, I would add, the Orthodox/ Muslim struggles in the Balkans and the religious three-way

(Catholic, Muslim, and Orthodox) wars in the former Yugoslavia in the 1990s.

Having said that, there is no doubt that for many of the participants on both sides of the conflict, their reasons remained firmly religious for the entire thirty-year period, and we should not forget that when we think of France's decision to act in a political rather than Catholic/Protestant manner.

In the fifteenth century, many Czechs, citizens of what was until 1918 called the kingdom of Bohemia, converted to the teachings of Jan Hus, the Bohemian reformer and martyr, who in retrospect (but not at the time) we would call a Protestant. Bohemia, like most parts of Central Europe, was ruled over by foreign kings who usually had much larger domains elsewhere, so that country was only one of many parts of their wider realms. (As a result, many non-Czechs lived in the kingdom, which until the seventeenth century also contained parts of what is now Germany and also Poland. The presence of the so-called "Sudeten Germans" in what became Czechoslovakia in 1918 was one of the causes of the Second World War.)

For a short while, the Bohemians had a Czech king, George Podiebrad, and during the fifteenth century they evolved what has been called Utraquist, a group that while Catholic in many respects allowed Holy Communion to be taken in a broader way than official Catholic teaching then allowed. By the seventeenth century, most Bohemians (which then included ethnic Germans and Poles as well as Czechs) were regular Protestants, but still used the Utraquist label for legal purposes, since Utraquist worship was permitted, albeit grudgingly, by the authorities.

So by 1618, therefore, Bohemia was a country that, since 1526, had been theoretically reigned over by Catholic Hapsburg kings, but which, unlike the more strictly Germanic parts of the Hapsburg realms, contained a very considerable number of Protestants, all of whom were able to worship freely.

The rest of Central Europe remained a tinderbox. In 1608, Protestant princes in what is now Germany formed a defensive military alliance called the Evangelical (or Protestant) Union—the German term *Evangelisch* usually just meaning Lutheran today, but referring to Protestants in general at the time. Head of this was the Calvinist elector palatine, one of the seven key rulers who helped to elect a Holy Roman Emperor. Frederick, who became elector palatine during this time, was also the son-in-law of the British king, James I, and it was hoped—incorrectly as it turned out, that if things developed badly, Britain would send troops to aid the German Protestant powers. Some mercenaries did in fact come to Frederick's palatinate, but unofficially and nowhere near enough to make any difference.

The electors palatine formed one branch of the ancient Wittelsbach dynasty—one that still exists today—the other one being that of the dukes of Bavaria. The latter were passionate Catholics, and, in the conflict that ensued, Duke Maximilian was to prove by far one of the ablest of all the German princes. But although they were Catholic, they also believed in the rights of princes as against any overweening power for the emperor, and that was eventually to become equally important. In 1609, Bavaria led the way to create a counterbalancing Catholic League, to offset the Evangelical Union, and now the empire was in two armed camps, and in a very dangerous position.

For, in 1618, there came a dynastic crisis for the Hapsburgs that in turn caused a spiritual and political crisis of epic proportions, first in Bohemia and then, for the next thirty years, with the most appalling military and sanguinary results in much of Europe.

Bohemia was not just an important kingdom, much bigger then than the Czech Republic is today. It also provided another one of the seven electors—the king held the electorship for Bohemia. In 1618, as there had been since the fourteenth century, there were seven electors: three ecclesiastical (Mainz, Trier, and Cologne) and four lay, or secular (Brandenburg, the palatinate, Saxony, and Bohemia). So long as Bohemia was held by a Catholic Hapsburg, his vote plus that of the three electoral archbishops meant that there was a permanent Catholic majority of electors, since all the other three secular electors were Protestants. Lose Bohemia to the Protestants, however, and the post of emperor would be captured at the next election by a Protestant, which, in Catholic eyes, would lead to disaster.

The previous year, the Diet of Bohemia had agreed that the heir to the Hapsburgs, Archduke Ferdinand of Styria (now a part of Austria) could be preelected as their king, the office still, in theory at least, being elective and not hereditary. The aged Holy Roman Emperor, Matthias, was childless, as had been his predecessor, Emperor Rudolf II, who had lived most of his reign as a recluse in Prague, more interested in the occult than in real life.

Rudolf and Matthias had been Catholics, but had not enforced the Counter-Reformation—the attempt to re-Catholicize Europe—with considerable vigor. Ferdinand, however, was a fanatical Catholic, trained by the Jesuits, the zealous missionary order that has been called the Shock Troops of Catholicism.

Matthias, having no direct male heir, had asked the Diet to preelect Ferdinand as their king. This they did in 1617, and then, by 1618, the Protestant majority suddenly realized the consequences—the full implementation, probably through the Jesuits, of the Counter-Reformation in Bohemia and the persecution of the Utraquist faith.

After much intrigue, the Bohemians eventually decided to elect a new king, a Protestant, and, in the mistaken belief that Britain would help, chose James's son-in-law, the elector Frederick. (To cut a long story short here, it is through his wife, Elizabeth, James's able daughter, that today's British Royal Family descends, since her youngest daughter, decades later, was to be the only Protestant heir of the Stuart dynasty. The unfortunate King George III and the present Queen, another Elizabeth, are her direct descendants.)

Frederick hesitated, and then foolishly accepted, without having enough military support to keep himself in power. Matthias died in 1619, and Ferdinand became the new Holy Roman Emperor. (Not recognizing Frederick as king meant that Ferdinand voted for himself, as the Catholics still, by his reckoning, had the 4:3 majority.)

One key thing we need to remember about this time—there were for all intents and purposes no regular, permanently existing, standing armies. Troops had to be raised specially—which cost money—and many rulers solved the problem by employing thousands of mercenaries, which cost even more money.

Frederick and Elizabeth spent the winter of 1619/20 in Prague, earning themselves the nicknames of the Winter King and Queen. But his forces were pathetically weak in relation to the armies that the emperor was soon able to raise. Although Frederick's forces did well initially, they were no match for the Catholic Imperial Army under the command of Count Tilly, once it finally geared into action.

(The Protestant elector of Saxony was a Lutheran not a Calvinist, and so disliked Frederick. Emperor Ferdinand was therefore able to bribe him with the Protestant, Germanic Bohemian province of Lusatia, which in due course became part of Saxony, and was lost to Bohemia for good. Other than Saxony, however, the war that now began was effectively Protestant on one side and Catholic on the other.)

In 1620, at the Battle of the White Mountain (sometimes called White Hill) just outside Prague, Tilly routed the meager Protestant armies. It looked as if the Czech rebellion was over and, with it, the Protestant cause in general, as Frederick not only had to flee Bohemia, but also lost his original palatinate possessions to his Bavarian cousins.

The Thirty Years' War is traditionally divided into phases,

the first three of which are, I would argue, essentially religious in nature, the last, from around 1635 to 1648, the first modern dynastic war, and not really religious at all.

Phase one was the original Bohemian rebellion, and its ruthless suppression. Ferdinand introduced the full blast of the Jesuit inspired Counter-Reformation to Bohemia. All Protestant nobles had their lands confiscated and given to Catholic families, often from outside the kingdom, who held them down to the twentieth century, when first Czechoslovak independence and then communism (after 1948) ended foreign domination. Bohemia went from being a mainly Protestant country to the Catholic country that the Czech Republic is today.

Phase two of the war need not concern us in great detail— but it does see the rise of the notorious Bohemian military commander, normally given the name Wallenstein, though Waldstejn is the correct Czech spelling. With commanders such as Wallenstein, Tilly, and Bernard of Saxe-Weimar on the Protestant side, Central Europe became like a wilderness. Mercenary armies needed money and food, and found it wherever they could, usually through pressure, plunder, rape, and murder, largely at the expense of towns and villages they invaded or occupied and then pillaged. For ordinary Czechs and Germans, these were to be thirty years of sheer unimaginable horror of a kind not seen again until the far worse carnage of the twentieth century.

So far it remained an essentially religious conflict. By 1629, it looked as if the emperor and the Catholic side were winning—they certainly had the full military advantage. Once Protestant realms such as Württemberg in the south and Mecklenburg in the north were now under Catholic martial occupation, and, in the Edict of Restitution that year, all Protestant gains of ecclesiastical property and territory since 1552 were forcibly given back to Catholic control, Protestantism, in its German heartland and place of origin, was now in a precarious state.

Then the war became internationalized, and Gustavus Adolphus, the Protestant king of Sweden, entered the war, as the "Lion of the North." In 1630, just as everything was looking desperate for the Protestant cause, foreign intervention changed the entire course of the war.

Until then, Gustavus Adolphus had spent much of his time fighting his Vasa dynasty cousins, who were kings of Poland and Catholic, from seizing back the Swedish throne for Catholicism. By 1630, it was safe for him to intervene in the chaos to his south, in the empire. This he now did, and with a vengeance.

The Swedish king had both a superb army of his own and excellent commanding abilities. Thus, in two years he swept through the empire and, by 1632, the situation was so transformed that it now looked as if the Protestants would win, and the Catholics not merely lose but do so badly.

Not only that, but Gustavus Adolphus, while himself a zealous and devout Protestant, who saw himself not just fighting for Sweden's interests, but that of Protestantism in general, had a very different idea of religious toleration from that which had existed hitherto in both Catholic and Protestant lands alike.

Remember *cuius regio eius religio*? We saw that while it looked good, it was of no help to, say, Catholics living in Brandenburg or Protestants in Bavaria. But when the Swedish armies occupied what had been Catholic territories during their great campaign through the empire, the king insisted that Catholics be allowed to continue to practice their faith freely. In other words, he was permitting *genuine* religious freedom and toleration, something that had not existed anywhere in Europe before.

Had Gustavus Adolphus prevailed, hundreds of thousands of lives would have been saved that were lost in sixteen more years of bloodshed—many if not most of them innocent noncombatant civilians. Genuine religious freedom would have become the norm. The subsequent history of Europe would have been far better, with incalculable consequences over the following centuries. Yet this was not to be.

In the first major battle between Gustavus Adolphus and the brilliant but cynical Wallenstein, at the Alte Veste, we can at best call the match a draw. Then, in late 1632, at the Battle of Lützen, the Swedish/Protestant forces won, but Gustavus Adolphus was killed in the fighting.

This now altered the war yet again. On the one hand, the Imperial/Catholic forces were no longer able to impose their will on the whole of Germany, and to force the Counter-Reformation upon those who would reject it—except in their own lands, such as in Austria and Bohemia, where Emperor Ferdinand imposed it ruthlessly. On the other hand, now that the charismatic and militarily able Swedish king was out of the picture—his successor on the throne was a young girl, Christina, who later abdicated, fled to Rome and converted to Catholicism—then the Protestants had no leader of their own to hold things together. All the gains they had made were undone, as the imperial forces were able to wrest many of them back, especially following the Battle of Nordlingen, a Hapsburg victory.

Historians call the part from 1635 to 1648 the "French phase." This is true, in so far as the main impetus against the Hapsburgs now came from France, the traditional and long-time adversary of that dynasty.

France was mainly Catholic, although many of its leading generals at this period, such as Marshal Turenne, were Huguenots. Its nominal king, Louis XIII and later the infant Louis XIV, did not at this time exercise much power, this being done first of all by Cardinal Richelieu as chief minister and real ruler, and later his successor, Cardinal Mazarin, who although ruler of France was in fact, by origin, an Italian.

In the same way that the Catholic Valois kings formed brief alliances with the Ottoman sultan to fight the Hapsburgs, now

Richelieu and Mazarin did the same with the Protestant princes in Germany, and with Sweden, to achieve the same ends. While for many of the local German Protestant rulers religion was still the main feature of the war, I think that one can now say that the *overall* war was no longer religious, but based upon the designs of both France and Sweden to benefit at the expense of the Hapsburg dynasty, which, we must remember, also had possessions in today's northern Italy as well as in Central Europe. Fighting broke out therefore on both fronts, and continued to do so until peace was finally achieved in 1648, in the Treaty of Westphalia.

Historians, political scientists, international relations specialists, and everyone else all agree, this time, that 1648 marks the watershed—the creation of the Westphalian System, that has, albeit in increasingly battered form, lasted down until our own day, and the rise of non-state-based extremist Islam. From now on, in the West at least, religion was no longer a motive for war, but territorial aggression and the rights of a nation state.

I would argue therefore that for our purposes, the history of religious warfare, we can say that in the West it ended in 1632, with the death of Gustavus Adolphus in battle. By the end of the seventeenth century the idea of toleration was becoming fashionable, and with the advent both of the Enlightenment— the "Enlightened Despot" Emperor Joseph II introduced it in his Hapsburg lands in the 1780s, for example—and then of the overtly secular French Revolution in 1789, religious toleration became the norm, certainly between different kinds of Christians, and, then, in a legal sense, for groups such as the Jews in the nineteenth century. Religious war was now a thing of the past. No more, too, would a government insist on the right to determine what you believed—or disbelieved—in the privacy of your own home.

All this is relevant to any discussion of Islam and its future direction in the twenty-first century. Many current commentators, especially those of a more liberal disposition, say that what Islam needs now is a Reformation. However, I believe, contrary to what most writers say, that in fact Islam *has* had a Reformation *already*, back in the eighteenth century, with the introduction of the Wahhabi version of that faith in the Arabian Peninsula. Wahhabism is the version of Islam that officially prevails in Saudi Arabia today, and is also the form of Muslim faith believed in not only by bin Laden and the 9/11 bombers, but by many, thanks to Saudi petrodollars, around the Islamic world today.

But whether or not I am right on that issue, the fact remains that the Reformation, however spiritually beneficial those of us of Protestant faith believe it to be (and in general too—many historians argue that the Enlightenment of the eighteenth century was only possible because of the Reformation), resulted in nearly a century of continuous warfare in Europe, in which parts of Germany lost over 60 percent of their population, and the Continent saw barbarities committed against civilians of a kind that had not been seen in centuries, even during the Middle Ages.

So, in wishing a Reformation on Islam, on the presumption that it has yet to take place, might we also be inflicting on that faith the same kind of internecine warfare that Christianity suffered in our Reformation period in the sixteenth and seventeenth centuries?

I ask because we now take for granted one of the results of the Thirty Years' War, between Catholics and Protestants in the heartlands of Europe, namely that religion is, as a result of all the carnage, no longer to be an issue of warfare between civilized states. This presupposes a post-1648, post-Enlightenment (i.e., eighteenth-century) separation of church and state that does not as yet exist in the Islamic world. They are for all intents and purposes at a juncture in their history akin to where we were in 1618, when the Thirty Years' War began. Once, not that long ago, we too had similar conflicts, and if we remind today's Muslims that the change we want to recommend to them is one we have made ourselves, they would, I hope, be more likely to listen to us—especially if, following Lamin Sanneh's line, modernity, tolerance, and freedom of thought and speech all have *religious* roots, and are not based upon a secular rejection of all religious views, Christian and Muslim alike.

❧ 5 ❧

THE POETRY OF GENOCIDE
Celebrating Religious Murder in Verse

EVER SINCE 9/11 in the United States and 7/7 in Britain, there has been a tendency in the West to regard the Muslims as perpetrators and Westerners as victims. We have seen in the previous chapters that for centuries the Islamic world was in fact on the offensive, with occasional Western sallies against the predominant Muslims during periods such as the Crusades, and then, after 1683, the boot was on the other foot and the West prevailed against a declining Muslim superpower, the Ottomans.

In this new century, the terrorists have been Islamic extremists, such as al Qaeda and its many affiliates. But one of the reasons they give for killing Westerners is that, in recent years, the main victims of warfare have been Muslims killed by Christians. If one considers the carnage of the Balkans in the 1990s, this is by and large true, although one should not forget that some of the victims were Catholic Croats killed by Orthodox Serbs, and, in 1995, Serbs killed in revenge by Croats. While 3,000 people, including some Muslims, were killed on 9/11, more than double the amount—8,000 men and boys—were slaughtered over the course of a few days in the massacre in 1995 in Srebrenica, and every single one of the victims were Bosnian *Muslims* butchered by Serb Orthodox irregular forces under the command of Ratko Mladic, a war criminal of epic proportions who, eleven years and more after the massacre, has still never been captured and handed over to justice.

In other words, the key thing to remember is that in our own lifetime, Muslims have been victims as much as perpetrators, and that the evil is by no means one sided. In this chapter therefore we shall mainly look at the way in which tens of thousands of Bosnian Muslims were slaughtered in the 1990s for no other reason than their religion, and then examine the smaller-scale instance of Muslims being butchered in India, this time by fanatical Hindu mobs, again solely because of their faith. Finally, we shall see what all this has to do with modern terrorism, and the excuses that such terrible massacres, in which Muslims are the victims, have given to the perpetrators of Muslim atrocities today.

This is the background, in a chronological sense, of the next phase in the story of religious warfare. In the West, by the end of the fifteenth century, Spain finally managed to recapture the Iberian Peninsula from Islamic rule—the *reconquista*, the seven-centuries-long saga of the slow and often spasmodic reconquest of Spain from the Moors, was finally over.

In the Eastern part of Europe in the same period, it was precisely the opposite story. When the Venetians and their allies so foolishly seized Constantinople in the Fourth Crusade, they opened the way for the various Muslim Turkish peoples living in Anatolia eventually to conquer the Byzantine Empire by 1453, end millennia of Christian rule, and begin upon the Ottoman conquest of the Balkan Peninsula and indeed of part of Central Europe itself. Had Vienna fallen to the Turkish siege in 1529, following the conclusive Ottoman victory over Hungary at Mohács in 1526, then the heartland of Europe would have been open to Islamic invasion for the first time since Charles Martel defeated the Muslim armies back in 711.

Up until now my chapters have been mainly chronological. In this one I break with that and for good reason: Except for the fanatical minority who want to restore Islamic rule to Spain—the kind of terrorist who committed the bombings in Madrid in 2003—we do not, by and large, live with the direct consequences today of the long period of Muslim rule in Spain, that ended over five hundred years ago. While moderate Muslims might feel nostalgia for the exceptionally gifted, highly artistic, and religiously tolerant Ummayad caliphs of Cordova even longer before, Muslim Spain has not caused twenty-first-century casualties.

The same, however, does not apply to the Balkans—in fact hundreds of thousands of innocent people, most of whom were Muslim, were annihilated in the twentieth century, right up until 1999, precisely because of events that took place in the Balkans six centuries and more ago. While for most the ghosts of El Andalaus are dead, those of parts of the Balkan Peninsula are very much alive. Alas, they are still claiming more victims to join their ghoulish ranks.

So this chapter will be a chronological mix, examining in part the Ottoman Turkish invasions of the Balkans from the fourteenth century onward, the conversion of many in that region to Islam, the faith of the conquerors, and the savage reactions to alien domination by many of the local peoples that has resulted in carnage for two to three hundred years or more, reaching a crescendo in events in the lifetime of most of us today.

Ottoman victory can be said to have begun, for all intents and purposes, at Manzikert, though it was their Seljuk ethnic cousins who won that victory. What the Turkish invasion of Anatolia did was to enable different Turkic tribes to settle in the region, and for a while diverse small kingdoms jostled with each other to be the most powerful.

One of the most famous Serbian poems is "The Mountain Wreath," one that noted writer Tim Judah has accurately described as a "paean to ethnic cleansing." Astonishingly, it is a poem written by a bishop, Petar II Petrovic Njegos, the leader of the Montenegrins, in 1847. It is based on a legendary raid just a few decades before, in the eighteenth century, by Montenegrin Serbs against Muslim Slavs. While other experts, such as Mark Mazower, doubt that the raid ever took place, one can say that since such raids did for certain take place in general, even if this one did not happen in particular, there were enough like it to give the poem a strong degree of authenticity.

It is, many Serb commentators agree, "the central work of all Serbian literature" (after the formation of Yugoslavia in 1918, of Yugoslav literature as well, this despite the fact that it glories in the slaughter of innocent Muslims).

I am concentrating on it not just because it shows Muslims as victims, though that is important enough in and of itself, but I am also doing so because it gives us an excellent insight into the terrorist mentality, and into that of twentieth-century mass killings, not just by Serbs and Croats against Bosnians, but by the Nazis and similar groups as well. This is the mind-set that produced the Holocaust, and indeed all genocidal massacres that took place in the twentieth century and beyond. In other words, this massacre, and the poem written to celebrate it, is the embodiment of religious warfare as we have seen it throughout our book.

The inspirer of the massacre was himself also a bishop, Bishop Danilo. Christmas Eve was approaching, and the bishop and his men decided to celebrate it by massacring as many of the Slavic Muslims as they could find. Since Christ himself survived a massacre—the Slaughter of the Innocents—just after being born, this was rather an ironic way of commemorating the birthday of the Prince of Peace!

Here we need to insert a little Balkan history—and here I have happily drawn on excellent books such as those by Tim Judah, Mark Mazower, Branimir Anzulovic, Vamik Volkan, Michael Sells and Misha Glenny, all listed in the bibliography at the back, along with my own academic work on this subject, *Why the Nations Rage: Killing in the Name of God.*

After the Ottomans invaded the Balkan Peninsula in the fourteenth century, they continued in the conquest up until they had captured most of Hungary as well, just under two centuries later. As with the earlier Islamic conquest of Spain, most of the inhabitants—Greek, Slavic, Albanian, Romanian and Hungarian alike—stayed Christian. However, a not insubstantial minority did not, converting to the religion of the new rulers, Islam.

Since hundreds of thousands of innocent men, women, and children were massacred in the period before the First World War, during the Second World War, and again in the 1990s, all because of who is supposed to have done what six hundred years before, in the fourteenth century, what might seem arcane and obscure to us in the West is of literal life-and-death importance in the Balkans in our own lifetime. Here it becomes historically very messy! (In lectures I have given on this, I referred to one group as the "boggling Bogomils," and I hope your mind does not boggle on what follows. . . . But it *is* comprehensible, so I trust you will persist.)

We have seen that invading Islamic armies, from the seventh century onward, did not try to enforce conversion on those they conquered—they kept to the Quranic injunction that "there is no compulsion in Islam." Some of this was financial—non-Muslims, who if monotheists were given protected or *dhimmi* status, had to pay more tax, and so revenue was higher from a Christian population than one that converted en masse to Islam.

However, on the other side, being *dhimmi* had strong disadvantages. Here, too, there is historical disagreement, as on all matters of Islamic (and Balkan) history. First, let us look at the system, and then at the argument on exactly how well all the differing religious groups in the Balkans—Muslim, Orthodox Christian, Catholic Christian, and Jewish—really got along with each other.

It is vital to keep in mind that in the Ottoman Empire, one's prime identity was *not* one's nationality but one's *religion*. The importance of this cannot be stressed too much. People were whatever religion they were born, and not only was that how the Ottomans saw people but also how people saw themselves. It is for this reason that the wars in the Balkans and all the massive carnage of the late nineteenth and of the twentieth century are *religious* conflicts, however incomprehensible such things might seem to us in the twenty-first-century West.

In a nutshell, everyone in the Ottoman Empire was part of the *millet* system. This categorized everyone, from grand viziers to humble peasants, entirely according to their religious affiliation. Muslims were in the Muslim *millet*, Jews in the Jewish *millet*, Catholics in their *millet*, and Orthodox Christians in the Orthodox *millet*, which, in the last case, owed political as well as spiritual homage to the Orthodox patriarch in Constantinople, who, as well as being a religious official was also appointed by the Ottoman sultans to keep an eye on the very large Orthodox population.

Most of the inhabitants of the Balkans were Orthodox, and it was this Orthodox faith to which they owed their allegiance. I think that such writers as Mark Mazower and those who agree with him are quite right to say that, until well into the nineteenth century, the average Slavic peasant thought of herself or himself as *primarily* Orthodox Christian, and that such modern, nationalistic ways of thinking of ourselves according to our ethnicity would have been quite alien to them.

Today there is an unusual agreement between the *bien pensant* politically correct liberal left and the British Thatcherite political right on the supposed tranquility of the Balkans, and for that matter, much of the rest of the empire, under Ottoman rule. Opposing such a lyrical view are historians on the religious right, such as the Islamic expert Ba't Ye'or (which is a pseudonym to protect her), who has written many books on the status of Christians under Islam, particularly those in the Middle East. In essence, the first side emphasizes how well every-

one got on, and the other how badly the Christians were oppressed. The politically correct assertion that Islamic rule was
always more enlightened than that under Christianity is well
known, and needs no introduction.

The Thatcherite defense comes from Lady Thatcher's strong
support of the Bosnians against the Serbs in the 1990s—including that of her ablest academic supporter, Brendan Simms—but
while I, too, more than sympathized with the Bosnians, and like
the Thatcherites and many in the United States was appalled at
the refusal of European powers to prevent the massacres, I have
reluctantly to say that even the ablest of Thatcherite historians
do not always have history on their side when it comes to how
the different groups lived together under Ottoman rule. Life in
Bosnia was not always a paradise; in the 1870s thousands of innocent Orthodox Bosnian Serbs were massacred not just by Ottoman soldiers but by Bosnian Muslim troops as well, in the
same way that equally horrific numbers of innocent Muslims
were slaughtered by Serb rebels back in 1804.

Here I agree with the proponent of a middle path, Mark
Mazower. In his history of the whole region, *The Balkans*, he
shows how hard it was for ordinary Christians to get on. Ca-
reers for non-Muslims were very limited, taxes were higher, and
there were genuine times of repression during which Christians
suffered particularly from whatever harsh edict was being imposed upon them for however long such decrees were in force.

However, in one of his other books, *Salonica: City of Ghosts*,
he looks at part of the Balkans in microcosm. (Salonica is the
old name for Thessaloniki.) Here he shows that in this one city,
Jews, Christians, and Muslims lived happily side by side for
centuries, right down until the twentieth century, when a combination of modern nationalism, and then Nazi genocidal ideology, made such tranquility permanently impossible—today's
Thessaloniki is an overwhelmingly Greek city.

In other words, the Balkans experienced not one extreme
or the other, but a mix of the two, with circumstances varying

considerably from place to place, often depending upon the whim of the local Ottoman officials.

But while most Balkan peoples stayed Orthodox (or Catholic and Protestant in Hungary, under its brief period of Ottoman rule), some did convert to Islam. As we saw earlier, Islam is a nonracial faith, which, like Christianity in its early centuries and again now from the twentieth, happily accepts converts of all races as full and equal members. This meant, for instance, that converted Slavs occupied some of the highest positions in the Ottoman Empire, and there were instances of a Slavic grand vizier not only negotiating on behalf of the sultan with an Orthodox Christian Slavic bishop, but the grand vizier and bishop were members of the same family. So for those Slavs who did convert, it was possible to gain any post within the empire, and also to become a major landowner or merchant, albeit, in the latter case, within the restrictions imposed by the Ottoman system of landholding.

The area where most conversions took place was in what is now Bosnia, and also Albania—though Muslims lived all over the Balkans for many centuries. It is here that the historical fun and games begin!

One of the key things that the Serbs were able to obtain for themselves, before the Ottoman conquests, is what is described as an *autocephalus* Church. This literally means "self-governing," and it meant that while Serbs were nominally under the patriarch in Constantinople, they also had their own national church: after the Ottomans finally conquered Serbia, in 1459—seventy years after the great defeat of the Serb armies at the Battle of Kosovo in 1389—they had a church that they could call their own. As it was the one remaining symbol of the once great Serbian empire, which at its peak ruled over large parts of what is now Greece and Macedonia, it helped keep the Serb national consciousness alive through all the five centuries and more of alien Ottoman rule.

Other areas of the Balkans also had their own Orthodox

churches, such as in what we now know as Romania, Greece, and Bulgaria. In these regions, though, the Greeks were dominant spiritually even if they were not ethnically; and historians have argued that this delayed national self-awareness in these regions until well into the nineteenth century.

With the Serbs, though, to be Orthodox was to be Serb and to be Serb was to be Orthodox. Religion and identity were every bit as tightly enmeshed as in the lands of Islam, in which church and state also went hand in glove, as they do today.

However—and this is where the complications come in—it was not quite so simple.

Back in the fourth century, the Eastern and Western halves of the old Roman Empire went in different ways, and, remarkably, the dividing line in the Balkans between what became part of the Byzantine Empire, and the rest, which stayed in the West, is still, in the twenty-first century, the dividing line between the Catholic and Orthodox parts of the Balkan Peninsula.

But while the *religious* dividing line is well over sixteen hundred years old, say, between Catholic Croatia and Orthodox Serbia, the same is not true ethnically. In fact, while the religious boundaries are visible, the ethnic borders are in reality far more confused. All depends on who converted to what in the fourteenth and fifteenth centuries, an historical debate that continues to mean literal life or death to thousands of Balkan inhabitants in recent times.

In Roman times, the area was inhabited by Illyrians, who are probably the ancestors of the Albanians today, along with descendants of Roman legionnaires who settled in the Balkans, from whom today's Romanians are said to descend (Romanian is a Romance language, like Italian or Spanish). In the era of the fall of Rome came two separate waves of Slavs, the northern half going to present-day Croatia, the southern to what is now Serbia.

Not a great deal is known about these particular invasions.

One of the problems is that much modern history is written by actively nationalist historians, who deliberately use the past to make points in the present, something we have already seen with regard to the historical accuracy of the accounts of early Islam. The Balkans are no exception, and, in any case, getting the truth at this vast historical distance would be a hard thing to achieve.

But the key point, I think, is that *ethnically speaking* we are not talking of two entirely different races but of two waves of invasion by the *same* race.

Linguistically, there was, until the 1990s, a language accurately called Serbo-Croatian. It was spoken by Serbs, Bosnians (of all descriptions), and Croats alike, the only differences being incredibly minor, such as that between the English spoken by a New Yorker and an inhabitant of San Francisco. Admittedly the Croats (and Bosnians) used the Latin alphabet and the Serbs the Cyrillic—the one used also in Russia and Bulgaria, but, for all intents and purposes, the language was exactly the same.

This is because, I would argue, along with others, that ethnically, Serbs, Croats, and Bosnians *are* all the same. *Ethnically* speaking, there is not a whit of difference between any of them. They may have entered the Balkans at slightly different times, and, historically, the Croats have never been under Muslim rule, having been conquered in the twelfth century by the Hungarians, and lived under continued Magyar rule until the twentieth century. Croats therefore became predominantly Catholic, as the Serbs became Orthodox, with a brief empire of their own under the mighty Nemanjic dynasty, and then under the Muslims until well into the nineteenth century—and in some parts of Serbia, into the twentieth.

You do not hear of Serbian Muslims, or Orthodox Croats. Yet we do hear of Bosnian Muslims, sometimes now described as Bosniaks. We also see Bosnian Serbs and Bosnian Croats. But why are they a people known by a religious, not an ethnic, appellation? This, too, was the source of tens of thousands of deaths in the 1990s, not to mention earlier massacres in the region, such as in the Balkan Wars of 1912–1913.

Their recent nomenclature—Bosnian Muslim—dates back as recently as Tito, the Yugoslav Communist dictator who ruled after the Second World War (Tito himself was half-Croat, half-Slovene). But most historians today would attribute their being described primarily as Muslim to the Ottoman *millet* system. The Bosnian Muslims of today are the descendants of those in the region we now call Bosnia who converted to Islam in the initial centuries after the Ottoman conquest in the fourteenth and fifteenth centuries.

This, tragically, is precisely why so many of them were massacred within our own lifetime. For while an independent Bosnian kingdom existed briefly in the twelfth and thirteenth centuries, and the Bosnians are, to most outsiders, a third Slavic group, politically but not ethnically distinct from the much larger Serbs and Croats, that is not how they were seen or are seen today by many of their powerful Serb and Croat neighbors.

To the Serbs, they were evil Serbs who played traitor to their Serb blood and converted from Orthodoxy to Islam. Similarly, to Croats, they were Croats who had been equally treacherous, and converted from Catholicism to Muslim faith. Just to confuse us all, many Bosnian Muslims claim that they in fact descend from a group of medieval Bosnians called the Bogomils. These were, like the Cathar Albigensians, the followers of a heresy linked ancestrally to the Zoroastrian religion, which entered the Balkans in a form similar to the Cathar heresy in southern France.

Historians of Bosnia, such as Noel Malcolm, and able recent defenders such as Brendan Simms, are surely right to say that the ancestors of today's Bosnian Muslims are in fact Bosnians, not Serbs or Croats. Again, at this distance, it is hard to tell, especially as the DNA of a Serb or Bosnian would be pretty much the same. I think here, too, I agree with the Western consensus that the Bosnian Muslims are in fact Bosnians who descended from another group altogether, namely Bosnians who were members of a local form of Christianity known as the Bosnian Church. Just to make matters interesting, little is known about this particular sect, except that it was Christian yet not entirely doctrinally in line with either the Catholics or the Orthodox. Religion, in other words, was not exactly strong in the Balkans, especially in Bosnia, and so when the Ottomans came, many local inhabitants did not possess strong enough Christian views to prevent them from converting to Islam. So while it is possible that some Bosnian Muslims do have Bogomil ancestry, it is far more probable that they simply descend from ordinary Bosnians who converted for a whole host of reasons to Islam centuries ago.

One likely historical fact, though, is wonderfully ironic, and would be funny but for so many having died as a result of religious identification in the Balkans over the years.

The irony is that, in older times, one was identified in that region as often by one's religion as anything else. It was not until the nineteenth century, when the winds of ethnic nationalism started blowing from Western Europe over to the Balkans, that many people even gave any thought to what ethnic group they actually belonged to. Many Bulgarians thought of themselves as Greeks, for example, because of their Greek Orthodox faith, something that still causes a problem with Macedonia, whom the Bulgarians think of as Western Bulgarians, the Greeks as Slavic-speaking Greeks and the Macedonians simply as themselves, Macedonians . . .

In the area, there were many of pre-Slavic origin. The two biggest groups were the Albanians, who no one mistook for anyone else as they were linguistically quite different, and the Vlachs (sometimes called Morlachs), who were an ethnic group not unrelated to the Romance language–speaking Romanians to the north.

It is the contention of many in the Balkans that the Bosnian

Serbs are not really Serbs at all, but Vlachs who converted to Orthodoxy, and ended up speaking the Serb language, in a way similar to the ancestors of the Bulgarians, many of whom were Turkic peoples who invaded the region in early times and then became absorbed into their Slavic surroundings. Needless to say, Bosnian Serbs—and Serbs in general—do not buy this particular interpretation of their past. But it does make sense if one recalls that in the *millet* system, everything revolved around one's religion.

We do not know what caused individual Bosnians to convert to Islam; perhaps it was genuine faith, or a desire to acquire the good things of life and turn to the religion of the new overlords. Whatever the motives were, and be they essentially religious or not, is not important. What does matter is that, in converting, they had identified themselves spiritually with the hated Ottoman oppressors, and for the Serb (or Vlach) population around them, that mattered a tremendous amount.

This is because the Serbs saw themselves as a holy nation, not unlike the Jews of Old Testament times, a promised race especially related to God, through suffering.

Two of the early Serb kings in the Middle Ages were saints—one a king who became one subsequently, and the other, Saint Sava, an especially holy and revered member of the Nemanjic ruling dynasty. (The most successful Nemanjic, King Stephan Dushan, was not made a saint as he became a king through murdering his father, and parricide was deemed to make him ineligible for sainthood.)

By the time of the invasion of the Balkans by the Ottomans, the great empire Stephan Dushan had so carefully put together had effectively disintegrated into many much smaller ruling factions and mini-states, none of which were powerful enough to resist the onslaught that now faced them. (Books by Noel Malcolm, Mark Mazower, John Fine, and Tim Judah tell the story so well we need not go into all the ins and outs of medieval Balkan history here.)

To cut a long story short, by 1389 the Ottomans had already conquered much of the Balkan Peninsula. Some states were in forced alliance with the Ottomans, and so when the tiny rump Serbia was invaded, there were Christian soldiers on the Ottoman side as well as Serb. The leader of the Serb army, Lazar, therefore had very little chance of success when the Ottomans engaged his forces at Kosovo Polje (the Field of Blackbirds), on the most sacred day in the Serb calendar, the feast of Saint Vitus, Vidovan.

While Serbs historically see Kosovo as a defeat, one could in fact argue that it was a draw, since the Ottoman sultan also lost his life, as well as Prince Lazar, and while the Serbs were forced to become Ottoman tributaries, it was not until 1459, a full seventy years later, that Serbia was fully conquered and placed under permanent Turkish rule until well into the nineteenth century.

Nonetheless, the Serbs, down to the present day, see 1389 as the most sacred and tragic year in their history. To us it seems rather strange that a nation would want so passionately to commemorate a defeat—as if the British celebrated Bunker Hill, or the French annually commemorated Waterloo! But bizarre as it sounds, that is indeed the case with the Serbs and Kosovo, even though history sees the battle as an even match and a shadowy Serbia survived two generations more.

Very soon after his death, Lazar became a sacred hero to the Serb peoples, a martyr who, to put it the Serb way, chose the heavenly realm rather than earthly glory. This expression, choosing heaven, is still a potent Serb catchphrase and mental concept; one that, for example, comforted many of the ethnic Serbs forced in 1995 by the Croats to evacuate the homes their families had lived in for centuries in the frontier Krajina area.

As the famous British archaeologist and discoverer of Knossos, Sir Arthur Evans, found in a tramp through the Balkans in the 1870s, bards still sang long tales of Kosovo, of heroic Serb self-sacrifice, of the heavenly realm. The same applied in the wars of the 1990s, and many reckon that it was the speech that the Serb leader, Slobodan Milošević, gave to the Serbs living in Kosovo, by this time a majority Albanian province, in 1989, that sparked off all the carnage of a few years later.

One important fact to remember when looking back at the 1990s, and before then to the many other massacres that broke out periodically in the Balkans from the late eighteenth century onward, is that some of the Balkan races were under Christian—mainly Hapsburg, some Venetian—rule, one group of Catholics ruling another, and also that some parts of the region, while under Islamic domination, never had remotely the violence that marked the wars in what is now the central and southern regions of the former Yugoslavia. This makes a huge difference to how we see the theme of this book, *religious* warfare.

The Catholic Croats were under the rule of Hungarian fellow Catholics, and the Slovenes, who were lucky in the 1990s to escape the bloodshed altogether, were also Catholics, under the rule mainly of Austrian Catholics, as were those Croats living in Dalmatia, who were first under Venetian Catholic rule, and then the equally Catholic rule of the Austrians. While no one likes being ruled by someone else, the cultural difference between, say, Croats and Hungarians was nothing like that between Christian Serbs and Muslims Ottoman Turks. Similarly, although Bulgaria had huge Muslim minorities—the Pomaks— right down to recent times, Bulgaria was able to escape the horrors of religious warfare. Also, while many Pomaks were expelled in the twentieth century and thousands of Christian Bulgars massacred by the Turks in the nineteenth, no one side ever sought to take bloodthirsty revenge upon the other.

In other words, as Mark Mazower reminds us, to see the Balkans as one giant sea of blood, gore, and violence is entirely mistaken. Furthermore, as many historians have correctly pointed out, no nation in southeast Europe can quite match the extreme violence of the Nazi period, where not just 6 million Jews perished in the Holocaust, but over 20 million Russians, whom the Nazis also regarded as racially inferior. We in the West have no right to lecture those living in other parts of the world, let alone those, to use one writer's phrase, in Europe's backdoor.

But from the eighteenth century on, and especially after the first stirrings of Serb revolt against Ottoman rule in 1804, carnage in the name of religion was certainly an integral part of the history of some parts of the Balkans, and it is this upon which we can now concentrate in greater detail.

The story of the "Mountain Wreath" was composed in the 1840s, and describes an undated massacre some years before. Yet if one looks at the phrases it employs, it could equally have been written in the 1990s, or, for that matter, of a Nazi massacre of Jews or Russians during the Second World War, for the worldview that it proclaims is exactly the same.

In the poem we see these Montenegrin Serbs as eighteenth-century ethnic cleansers who took the "extermination of the Turkifiers" to its very literal and horrifying conclusion. (I am following the same translation that I used in my book *Why the Nations Rage*: see the footnotes in that work for precise bibliographical details.)

Bishop Danilo starts the process by saying:

The blasphemers of Christ's name
We will baptize with water or with blood!
We will drive the plague out of the pen!
Let the song of horror ring forth,
A true altar on a bloodstained rock.

The goal is to "cleanse" the country of infidels. Here the word employed is *cestici*, which is strictly speaking an anachronism, as the term was not employed until the first uprising against the Turks in the period 1804–13. It literally means the extermination of unwanted parts of the population. The pen is a pig pen—until some way into the nineteenth century pig farming was one of the main sources of revenue in this part of the Balkans.

Here we can see the psychology of such acts. Getting rid of someone who is Not-Us is a classic psychological act, expelling those alien to oneself, even though they might be a tiny percentage of the population, or entirely innocent of any wrong doing to one.

This perspective recurred later in the light of the Romanian fascist desire to purge their country of Jews in the twentieth century, which is relevant to our purposes as the Iron Guard did so specifically in the name of Christianity, the League of the Archangel Michael, and notwithstanding that Romanian Jews were a considerably smaller part of the population than were the Jews of Nazi Germany.

This kind of thinking prevailed in the Balkans down to recent days—the desire, for example, to murder as many Bosnian Muslims as possible, to annihilate Muslim Kosovar Albanians, and to make Serbia an entirely ethnically/religiously Serb zone.

It is also identical to al Qaeda's desire to get rid of Americans from the sacred land of Arabia—although American troops were a minute percentage of the population, the term that bin Laden uses about them is very similar to the language employed by Bishop Danilo here about bin Laden's coreligionists, the local Slavic Muslims, which of course makes the 1998 statements rather ironic, as extremist Muslims of our era would not wish to think they were mentally identical to those who murdered innocent Muslims three centuries earlier.

In the poem, the Muslims are likened, just as in bin Laden's 1998 fatwa, to a plague. Plagues are by definition evil and must be removed. Reducing your enemies to bacillus status of course dehumanizes them and makes them easier to kill—we don't normally go around slaughtering fellow humans, but we do not hesitate to rid ourselves of diseases, especially those as serious and harmful as a plague.

The other thing to note is that it is religious language used. As experts such as Mark Juergensmeyer, of the University of California, have pointed out, this is to render ordinary human conflicts into a bigger, cosmic dimension, and to make it possible to give divine sanction to what would otherwise be, in this and many similar instances, just plain murder in any other context. Normally one does not go around killing people, but if God says so, then it must be all right—or so the twisted logic goes. Again, it depersonalizes the massacre—it is not one person committing a barbarous act, but a whole group executing the will of God. They are not personal enemies, but the enemies of God, who must therefore be obliterated in response to heavenly decree.

The massacre begins on one Christmas Eve:

There's slaughter and a big one, too
Delighted and I listened to it for one hour.

Those who had carried out the slaughter proudly tell the Bishop:

As large as the Cetinje valley is,
Not a single witness escaped
To tell what happened there.
We put our sabres under all those
Who did not want to be baptized,
But those who bowed to the Holy Child,
And crossed themselves with the Christian Cross,
We accepted as our brothers.
We burned all Turkish houses
That there may be no abode or trace
Of our infidel domestic enemy.

The Bishop was thrilled to hear of the carnage:

What a great joy my falcons,
What a joy, heroic liberty!
This morning you've marvelously resurrected
From the tombs of our forefathers.

Still more innocent Muslims were butchered elsewhere:

The slaughter lasted one day and a night,
The Crimnica River was filled with Turks.
There is no longer in our district
Any trace of the Turkish presence
Except for the headless corpses and ruins.

Tim Judah has commented on the way in which this poem
was an inspiration to late generations. Using a different English
translation, he shows how the murderers of over 8,000 Bosnian
Muslims at Srebrenica in 1995 used exactly the same method-
ology to annihilate their victims, and the identical psychology.
Everyone and everything had to be destroyed, so that there
would be no trace, no witnesses, and no survivor to tell tales. A
young bus driver had bravely wanted to help at least some
Muslims to escape. But the soldiers insisted that even the bus
drivers be complicit in murder, and had to kill at least one Muslim. When the poor driver asked if he could help any escape,
military orders came back: "The boss doesn't want a single witness left behind us." As Judah remarks, this is identical to what
happens in "The Mountain Wreath":

No single seeing eye, no tongue of Turk,
Escap'd to tell his tale another day!
We put them all unto the sword . . .

The massacre that the poem describes probably only killed
hundreds rather than the thousands or tens of thousands of
subsequent genocidal massacres.

What is significant, as Judah and other writers point out, is
that it is *Slavs* being murdered, *not* Turks. Admittedly, in the

first Serb uprising in 1804, thousands of actual Turks were either slaughtered or forced to flee, especially from the area around Belgrade. But we know that the victims in the poem, and in most of the actual, historically authenticated massacres since, right down to our own times, were all Slavs, the identical ethnic group to those committing the atrocities.

Some politically correct commentators dislike the idea that this really was all about religion. The best exponent of this view is probably Michael Ignatieff, a former BBC commentator, Harvard professor, and now a member of the Canadian Parliament. In his otherwise superb book on the Yugoslav carnage in the 1990s, *Blood and Belonging*, an excellent account of the new kind of savage nationalism that reemerged post-1989, he downplays the role of religion in the mayhem that took place.

I think that, by contrast, Tim Judah and countless other writers, such as Paul Mojzes, have it right, and that we *are* talking about religion-based war. Above all, Michael Sells describes what happened in the 1990s as entirely based upon religious, rather than ethnic, differences in his superb *The Bridge Betrayed: Religion and Genocide in Bosnia*. He shows that the only real differences among the Serbs, Croats, and Bosnians are in fact religious, since they are in all other respects the same, and that to say *ethnic cleansing* is in fact therefore technically incorrect. Ethnically all three nationalities are identical—the "cleansing," in fact, as he points out, a euphemism for murder, is thus *religious cleansing*, since religious differences alone determined whether or not someone was murdered in the death camps, such as the infamous one that the Serbs established at Omerska, which gained international notoriety when television journalists discovered it in 1992.

I agree also with writers such as Judah who say that it was the *religious* element of Ottoman rule that made the key difference in the Balkans, that it was *Islamic* domination rather than simple Turkish imperialism that created the problem.

Both he and Sells (and others) are thus right to say that this

is what made the religious elements of strife so peculiarly vicious in the Balkans, especially from the Serb revolt in 1804
onward. Civil wars are by their very nature especially cruel—
people who have lived for ages cheek by jowl now killing one
another, as Michael Ignatieff reminds us in several helpful illus-
trations—and the added religious dimension in the Balkans
made them worse still.

This is because the Slavic Muslims were seen as special trai-
tors—they spoke the same language as their fellow Christians,
they often dressed the same, they lived in the same or neighboring towns and villages, yet they or their ancestors had converted to the religion of the hated enemy and oppressor, the
Ottoman Turks.

This is why generations of Serbs onward would refer to
their Muslim fellow Slavs not as such but as "Turks." They
were not Turks, of course, but it was as if in changing their religion they had changed their whole ethnic as well as religious
identity as well—what Michael Sells (and I) have referred to as
religious nationalism. Religious and national self-identity become
fused into one, so that those of a particular ethnic group must
also be members of a defined religion, otherwise they are not
true members of that ethnicity, even if they are so biologically.

This is not unfamiliar territory. We saw this fleetingly when
we considered the Wars of Religion in sixteenth-century France,
when most French people felt that to be authentically and pa-
triotically French, it was necessary also to be a Catholic. This
was similar, but without the violence associated with it, to the
situation in England from the reign of Queen Elizabeth I onward, when the dictates of patriotism decreed that loyal English people were Protestants, especially since so many of the
nation's enemies, such as France, were overwhelmingly Catholic
in composition. The presence of minorities—Huguenot Protestant in France, Catholic in England, was not something that
could be tolerated, however small that minority might be.

It was thus the same in the Balkans, but made far worse by

the fact that there we are talking of altogether different religions, Muslim and Christian. Croat Catholics disliked Hungarian rule but were fellow Catholics, and in England, although the Catholic minority had a hard time, not gaining civil rights until the 1820s, nonetheless England was a Protestant country ruled by Protestants, whereas the Serbs were a majority Orthodox people ruled by people who were foreign twice over, ethnically as Turks and spiritually as Muslims.

In the Yugoslav wars of the 1990s, a young Serb fighter met a *Washington Post* journalist, and told him that he had "cut the throats of three Turks and I don't even have nightmares." (Reading this, Senator Daniel Patrick Moynihan felt obliged to respond that barbarity had truly returned. . . .)

The victim was in fact no Turk but a Bosnian Muslim. Seeing one's enemies as something that they—and one—are not also makes it easier to kill them, and here the dehumanizing process embodies this twice over—they are *Turks*, in other words, not a fellow Slav, and they are thus Muslims, and therefore not a Christian Orthodox believer.

Sometimes there were actual Turk victims; this occurred, in two wars, one fought in the 1870s, when Turkish and Slavic Muslims joined together to attack Bulgarian, Serb, and other rebels who had revolted against Ottoman rule. Here the Ottoman forces, the *bashi-bazouks*, butchered thousands of innocent Christian Slavs, in what the outraged British statesman, William Gladstone, described as the "Bulgarian atrocities."

The other vicious campaign was that of the First Balkan War in 1912, when the Greeks, Bulgarians, Serbs, Romanians, and others joined together to recapture as much of the remaining Balkans as possible from Ottoman rule. In this instance, both sides carried out hideous atrocities, and those against civilians, who suffered in enormous numbers, were of course the worst of all. The Greek soldiers were told not to regard the Turkish soldiers as even being human—a similar concept to the way in which German troops regarded Russian soldiers as less than human *Untermenschen* during World War II—and that helped in the general process of desensitizing the Greek soldiers in regard to Turkish casualties.

In the 1912–13 First Balkan War, the Croats played no role as they were still under the rule of the Hungarians. But the Serbs were most active, and Serbia was highly successful in capturing large swathes of territory, including their former historic heartland of Kosovo. But now, centuries later, comparatively few Serbs lived there, and the majority of the inhabitants, then as now, were Muslim Albanians—fellow Europeans, but not believers in Orthodox Christianity.

As the Carnegie Commission reported on the war not long afterward, the rage of Serb soldiers against innocent Albanians was horrific—just as it was to be years later when so many equally blameless civilian Albanians were slaughtered in 1999. The Commission noted that Serb soldiers "unleashed the full force of nationalist hatred against defenceless villages." In one particular scene for which they obtained witnesses:

> Burning was going on all around us . . . Albanian villages had been turned into pillars of fire. For two days before . . . [the witness's] arrival in Skopje the inhabitants had woken up in the morning to the sight of . . . heaps of Albanian corpses with severed heads.

These were, it transpired, the victims of Komitadjis, Serb irregular forces better known in the Second World War and in the 1990s conflicts by their alternative name of Chetniks. The witness continued that other corpses floated down the river to their location in the town. But the key thing was that what "was clear was that these headless men had not been killed in battle." They were innocent civilians slaughtered for their different faith.

The commission also noticed that what we now call ethnic cleansing had happened. As they put it, they had seen:

Houses and whole villages reduced to ashes, unarmed and innocent populations massacred en masse, incredible acts of violence, pillage and brutality of every kind — such were the means that were employed and are still employed by the Serb-Montenegrin soldiery, with a view to the ethnic transformation of [these] regions.

However, it should also be said that, as in the 1870s, the Ottomans were also carrying out equally barbaric actions against the equally innocent Christian Greek and Slavic civilian populations. As the commission observed, eyewitnesses saw:

Everywhere, bodies reduced to mere bones, blue hands ripped from their forearms, the bizarre gestures, empty sockets, open mouths calling as if in desperation, the shattered teeth behind the torn and blackened lips.

The Carnegie Commission also noticed that, in addition to the ethnic cleansing and mass murder, it was also the norm to torch the entire village:

The burning of villages and the exodus of the defeated population is a normal habit and traditional incident of all Balkan wars and insurrections. It is a habit of all these peoples.

I think that religion and religious difference is an important rationale behind such horrors. As we saw even in the desire of French people not to have Protestants living on their land during the Wars of Religion, and with the wish of Germans in the twentieth century to have a *judenrein* (Jewish-free) state, those for whom religion becomes pathological, such as al Qaeda's wish for only true Muslims to live within the Arabian peninsula, cannot cope with those exactly unlike themselves being even in physical proximity, however small the group unlike them might be.

Ottoman troops were to commit atrocities on a truly genocidal scale just a few years later, from 1915 onward, when *millions* of Christian Armenians were slaughtered in what many
now, correctly, regard as the first Holocaust of the twentieth
century. I am writing this in the week that the brave Turkish
author Orhan Pamuk won a well-deserved Nobel Prize for Literature, a merited reward for someone who has always insisted
that the Armenian genocide *did* take place, and that Turks were
responsible, in a Turkey that still, in the twenty-first century,
wishes to deny that any such events took place.

During the Second World War, the artificial Yugoslav state
that had been constructed after 1918 broke up once more, but
this time by force, at the hands of the Nazi German and Italian
invaders (with Bulgaria and Hungary also seizing some territory). The Croats were given independence, but the Croat state
also included most of Bosnia-Herzegovina. What developed
was a triple war: Croat (or Ustaše) and Bosnian Muslim fas-
cists collaborating with the Germans and Italians, mainly at the
expense of the Serbs; Serb forces, the Chetniks loyal to the ex-
iled king fighting both the Axis forces and the Communists; and
a genuinely Yugoslav but Communist Partisan army, led by
Tito, that mainly fought the Axis, but also the Chetniks.

Britain originally supported the Chetniks, but then, very
controversially, when they discovered that Tito was doing the
real fighting against the Axis, supported his Partisans instead.
The result was a Partisan victory, and the re-creation of Yugoslavia in 1945, under Communist rule. Tito died in 1990, and
with the strong man gone, the artificial state began once more
to unravel, with warfare breaking out in 1991 when the Slovenes
and Croats, followed by the Bosnians a little later, declared
their independence.

During World War II, Tito tried hard to create a genuine,
interethnic, interreligious sense of Yugoslav nationality—known
by him and the communists as Brotherhood and Unity. This,

Tito knew, was important because so many large-scale atrocities had been committed during the 1941–45 period. Here the main fighting was not in fact Muslim/Christian, since many of the Muslims fought together with the Catholic Croats against the Orthodox Serbs, with Croat fascist Ustaše forces being sometimes *so* barbaric that even the German SS forces were shocked. In addition, the Croats also tried to force many Serbs to become Catholic, and forced conversions were common. However, the Serb Chetnik forces, and Tito's own Partisans, who were drawn from all the ethnic and religious groups, also committed atrocities of their own, and especially against each other.

Tito did his best to keep Yugoslavia together, not an easy task, since memories of all the atrocities that took place during the war did not vanish but were simply suppressed, until times changed. Some of his subjects—with numbers of whom I spent many happy holidays in the 1970s and 1980s—genuinely regarded themselves as Yugoslavs, and whatever their nationality or religion (if they had any of the latter) as very much secondary. For others, they were still very much Croat, or Bosnian, or whatever the case might be.

In addition, Tito recognized the Bosnian Muslims as a distinct group of their own, with their own legal identity. They were the biggest single group within their state, Bosnia, but never over 50 percent of the population, as many Croats and Serbs lived in the region, as their ancestors had also done for centuries. So while, for example, all looked wonderful when the Winter Olympics happened in Sarajevo, and everyone applauded what looked like interreligious, interethnic harmony, the outside appearance was in fact deceptive.

After the breakup of the Yugoslav state from 1991, venomous rows erupted in both the academic and wider communities as to exactly how many people had been slaughtered, when, and by whom, during the war. Was it tens of thousands at X, or hundreds of thousands, and who did the killing and why? Since the disagreement depended almost entirely on the nationality of the protagonists, it is by now impossible to tell exactly who is right—all we can say for certain is that hundreds of thousands of entirely innocent people were massacred, and that Tito's achievement in keeping such disparate groups together after 1945, until he died in 1980, was an amazing achievement.

One of the main difficulties he had is that atrocities were remembered as if they had happened only the previous afternoon, let alone decades before. The other problem was that mass killings that had occurred *centuries* before were also recalled as if they had taken place that week, or that very day. Serb anger at Kosovo, way back in 1389, burned indignant even though Serbia had regained its independence in the 1850s, and was by far the biggest and most powerful constituent parts of the Yugoslav state after 1918 and then post-1945.

So consequently, when war broke out again in 1992, with Croatian and then Bosnian independence, it was the third time in the twentieth century in which interreligious carnage was taking place, with civilians as the main casualties.

Here I should say I do not subscribe to the "ancient hatreds" excuse used by many European statesmen after 1992, that said that all these Balkan peoples were a bunch of savages who had been slaughtering each other since time immemorial, and that the less neighboring European countries did to get involved the better. Allowing hundreds of thousands of civilians to be murdered or "ethnically cleansed" right on your doorstep was surely an immoral thing to do, and I agree fully with the consensus in America—with Republicans such as Bob Dole agreeing with Bill Clinton—that the West had to intervene to stop the carnage, which the Americans did at Dayton in 1995.

Nevertheless, while most Balkan peoples have lived together happily for centuries, and the Croats, under Hungarian rule until 1918, have no prior record of mass murder, one cannot avoid the fact that when it comes to Christian–Muslim interaction, mutual slaughter and killing has been going on for at least two hundred years, which makes those particular hatreds certainly old, even if not actually ancient.

For as soon as war erupted in 1992, the massacre of innocent civilians began all over again.

Here I agree with what many in the U.S. government have said on and off the record: of all the scores of massacres and atrocities in the Balkans in the 1990s, the Serbs are probably guilty of at least 70 percent, the Croats of around 20 percent (against both Bosnian Muslims in towns such as Mostar and against the Kraijina Serbs in 1995), and the Bosnians of around 10 percent—the right-wing supporters of the Bosnian Muslims who claim that this last group was totally innocent does not tie in with a great deal of impartial outside evidence to the contrary.

Having said that—and it is important to remember that several massacres, such as the one by Croat irregulars against Bosnian Muslim civilians that British troops discovered at Ahmici, for instance—were *not* Serb, all the major mass murders and long-term atrocities were without doubt carried out by Serb soldiers and their local allies.

Furthermore, as many witnesses at the time made clear, it *was* religious. Take for example a typical massacre committed by Serb soldiers on May 3, 1992, at the Bosnian village of Hranca. Here Serb militiamen—irregular, part-time soldiers who had until recently been ordinary civilians—torched all the houses and murdered nearly all the inhabitants.

The British journalist Tim Judah found one of the very few survivors, a woman.

Near the house, pools of drying blood were still visible where they had been killed.

"Why? Why? You ask why?" screamed a woman, tears streaming down her cheeks. "There is no food or drink . . . all our stores are burned. They want to ethni-

cally cleanse this area . . . There is no why . . . it is because
we are Muslims."

I think that this is a correct analysis. It is also what Freud
called the "narcissism of minor differences," a phrase picked up
by writers on the Balkan wars such as Sells and Ignatieff. This
woman's relatives had been slaughtered because they were
Muslims, and thus of the same religion of the centuries-long oppressors of the Serb murderers.

While mass killing and burning were, as the Carnegie Commission had rightly observed back in 1913, par for the course
in such gruesome Balkan conflicts, there was another element
added in the 1990s that had not been quite so prevalent before,
at least not in the region's domestic religious wars. This was deliberate rape—rape as policy.

In wars, rapes has often taken place and on a mammoth
scale. Perhaps the best known example was the wide-scale
rape—often combined with murder—of millions of German
women by Soviet troops after their conquest of Germany in
1944–45. This is not to say that Allied troops were altogether
innocent, but German people noticed that—while there were
some instances on the Western Front, with British and American troops—on the Eastern Front, the one with the Soviets,
such atrocities took place on an industrial scale.

Initially the rapes, along with large-scale looting, were neither condemned nor condoned by the Soviet authorities. The
troops, Stalin notoriously admitted, needed some fun. The ex-
tent of the carnage on the Eastern Front—maybe 20 *million* or
more died, many of these being Russian civilians, including Soviet Jews, wiped out by the Nazis—made that part of the war
probably the most brutal ever conducted in the history of warfare itself. So as well as the usual excuse of sexual release, there
was without doubt a powerful element of revenge in the
thoughts of the Soviet perpetrators. But then many Red Army
men raped their female comrades, without any of the excuses

available. Not only that, but of course the German women attacked were innocent, except by way of shared nationality, with their menfolk who had committed the atrocities against the Russians since 1941. Rape is never excusable, whatever justifications the Soviet leadership initially gave.

Eventually the Soviet authorities realized, as John Lewis Gaddis and other writers who have read the Soviet archives have now revealed, that this was likely to create a terrible reputation for the USSR among those Germans over whom the Russians were now going to rule, following the end of war allocation of zones of occupation. Gaddis has in fact gone so far to argue, with considerable merit, that this act of Soviet barbarity meant that to most Germans, the DDR, the Soviet puppet regime in East Germany, never had the legitimacy in the eyes of its ordinary citizens because of what it had revealed about the true, despotic nature of the Soviet regime.

However, although the Soviet authorities had initially winked at the deeds of their soldiers, no Soviet rapist did so under direct orders from the Kremlin.

This was entirely different with the mass rapes committed against Muslim women by Serb soldiers and irregular forces in the 1990s—what is truly horrific is that, apart from the vileness of the actual deed itself, rape was official Serb policy against Bosnian Muslim women, not just to humiliate them in a display of male power, but also to make sure that they were impregnated by Serb men. A child thus born would, according to Serb racial and religious ideology, be born Serb Orthodox and not Bosnian Muslim, and the Bosnian Muslim race would thus be outbred and ethnically/religiously cleansed from the Balkans.

As University of Virginia psychologist Vamik Volkan has written about these atrocities, this is bad biology, quite apart from being war crimes. But this dogma, however inaccurate, was nonetheless sincerely believed by the thousands of Serb soldiers who raped their way across the Balkans.

It was mainly the state-sponsored rapes in Bosnia that

gained world media attention. But the policy continued right up until 1999, when Serbs attacked the Kosovar Albanian population as well, until, this time, rescued by NATO intervention.

A classic example of the whole phenomenon can be seen in what happened in Kosovo, in the region of Qirez, that year. All six villages were torched, and their inhabitants forced to flee. Up to 70 percent of the wells were deliberately contaminated with dead bodies, to make the area permanently uninhabitable.

Thankfully there were a few survivors. But theirs was a gruesome, horrific tale. As a group of them told the Center for the Protection of Women and Children:

> Rape was one of the weapons of war that was used against women and young girls. Many men are still missing and no one knows their whereabouts. One woman from the village of Kochice was killed in front of her children. Three people have been burned alive . . . This village has twenty people killed (among them one child and five young women who have been raped before being killed and thrown into water wells) . . . These young women were raped by sent forces, later killed . . . There are rumours that some raped women were thrown into the wells alive.

Muslim society is very honor based, and rape is thus a source of shame not only to the woman, but also to her extended family and sometimes to the whole village or wider community. In some Islamic countries—such as happens in parts of Pakistan today—the woman victim is, herself, punished for committing adultery, even though she was raped and there was no consent. Pregnancy outside of wedlock is a source of particular shame, and a woman who is raped and thus made pregnant is doubly shamed. All this was well known, of course, to the Serb perpetrators.

During the rapes—they were even "rape camps" where they were carried on en masse—a Bosnian woman at one of them, near Prijedor, was told that she and the other victims "were going to give birth to Serbian children." At another similar camp, near Doboj, one woman told how "women who got pregnant . . . had to stay there for seven or eight months, so they could give birth to a Serbian kid." By this means, the Serbs would replace the Bosnians, and Serbia would again rid the Balkans of its Muslim inhabitants.

Feminists writing about these rapes knew therefore that this was not just "pressure-cooker rape" of the kind that tragically often happens in war, but something far worse, not simply a crime against women but a deliberate act of genocide — against a whole group.

(Similar rapes took place, I have read, in very different circumstances, in the Pakistani attempt to suppress the Bangladeshi rebellion in 1971 — here the key difference was that the two groups were *ethnically different* but *religiously the same* — Pashtun men raping Bengali women, but with both the Pakistanis and Bangladeshis being of the same religion, Islam.)

As the distinguished American feminist writer Catherine MacKinnon has expressed it, this was:

> ethnic rape as an official policy of war, in a genocidal campaign for political control . . . rape as an instrument of forced exile, rape to want to make you leave your home and never come back.

As various reports recognized, campaigns of mass extermination in the Balkans were not new: the Carnegie Commission noted in 1913 that the wars were worse for being among people who had lived together as civilians before the conflict. These were conflicts "waged not only by armies but by nations themselves . . . This is why these wars are so sanguinary, why they . . . end with annihilation of the population and the ruin of whole regions." For the perpetrators, the commissioners noted, the goal was the "complete extermination of an alien population."

In the 1990s rape was part of this same process. As a UN report noted in 1995 on the rape issue:

> The vast majority of victims were Muslims, and only Serb nationalists committed rape as part of a comprehensive countrywide scheme of terrorism known as ethnic cleansing.

What is also strange about the rape of Muslim women—Catholic Croat women managed to escape such horror, though thousands of Croats were killed or ethnically cleansed—is that it was also seen as a revenge for something quite different that the Turks had done centuries before.

This was the *dervshime* system that we saw earlier. It is well established that the Ottomans were not racist—so long as one was a Muslim one could hold even the very highest office, grand vizier included. Many high officials were, for example, European Slavs or African by ancestry—white or black mattered not a whit. What counted was being a Muslim, and this was essential, except perhaps in diplomatic posts, in which Greek Orthodox subjects of the empire were often employed, as translators or ambassadors, especially in negotiation with Christian countries.

At the same time, the Ottomans wanted a cadre totally loyal to them as individuals, owing no allegiance to anyone else. For this reason, they resorted to the large-scale kidnapping of boys from Christian homes—Slavs from the Balkans, Circassians from the Caucasus—who would be taken to Istanbul, converted to Islam and made into either soldiers loyal only to the sultan (the corps of janissaries) or into civil servants, the *dervshime*.

Vamik Volkan has argued, I think convincingly, that for some Serbs at least, the rapes were a kind of revenge for the way in which Ottoman Turks, centuries before, had stolen young Slavic boys from the villages and turned them into Muslims soldiers or civil servants. This seems very strange to us, and, of course, the Bosnian women so barbarically treated in the twentieth century were not in any way responsible for the deeds of Ottoman sultans hundreds of years before they were even born.

Whether this also applies to the majority of Serb rapes of Bosnian women is not so sure, though it undoubtedly influenced some, including those investigated by Volkan. However, the system of kidnapping to provide loyal administrators was without question part of the overall sense, centuries long, of Serbian humiliation at the hands of religiously alien rulers, and *that* was surely part of the reason for deep hatred of the fellow Slavs in Bosnia who went over to the religion of the enemy.

While women were by far the majority of the victims, some Bosnian Muslim men were also forced to bite off the testicles of fellow Bosnian Muslim prisoners, again as part of a desire to wipe out the propagation of future Muslim inhabitants of the Balkans. As noted earlier, even bus drivers were forced to be part of atrocities, so that as many Serb men as possible would be complicit in the violence that took place against the Bosnians.

There is, according to many experts, strong logic behind this, barbaric though it might seem to us.

During the 1990s, there was much talk in the newspapers of "senseless violence." However, what is senseless to decent people sitting reading the news in New York, Chicago, or Los Angeles is in fact very sensible to others with a radically different mindset from, say, Pale or Belgrade.

If we are ever to deal effectively with the threat of terrorism, we need to understand that millions of people around the world think in an entirely different way from us; and unless we begin to see fully how *they* understand things, we are never going to get very far in dealing with the issues facing us in the twenty-first century. The same applies to how we see terrorist activities committed by those not in fact unlike us, by white Europeans, millions of whose ethnic kindred live in the United States, and who are therefore far closer to us than we might like to admit. What follows is my imaginary tale, based upon some real places, and using writer Mark Hechter's ideas (and similar stories from others) as the basis.

Let us say, for example, that there are two neighboring villages, *X* and *Y*. X is filled with Bosnian Serbs, who are Orthodox, and Y with Bosnian Muslims, who follow Islam. Traditionally, these two villages have got along together fine, despite their two differing faiths. X has a large Orthodox church, and Y contains a mosque that dates back to the fifteenth century.

War breaks out. The inhabitants of X and Y become more nervous in relation to each other, but still manage to get along—just. They now phone each other instead of intervisiting physically—it would not be helpful to get caught in the wrong village if trouble erupts.

Tragically for all, the idyll is shattered when the Serb Tigers, under their notorious gang leader, Arkan, arrive in X, the Serb village. They force at gunpoint all the young men to come with them, and they then torch and massacre everyone male in Y, the Bosnian Muslim village. The women, those who survive, are taken away to one of the rape camps. The mosque is razed to the ground—according to the Serb way of thinking, it is an essential part of the history of Balkan Islam, and therefore, like the far more famous Bosnian Muslim library and archive in Sarajevo, it must be destroyed altogether, since that way the memory of the Bosnian Muslims can be eradicated from the region, as well as all the people themselves. To destroy the symbols of the enemy is as important as killing the enemy itself. (Those wanting more on this can read the many excellent but very academic books by British sociologist Anthony Smith, who deals superbly with the symbolism of ethnic and religious memories, from ancient times down to the present. Symbology is a genuine science, not just something invented by Dan Brown for his hero in *The Da Vinci Code*!)

Arkan and his men then tell the quaking inhabitants of X that as some of the young men from the village have taken part in the massacre of Y—however unwillingly—the whole village is thus responsible for all the atrocities that the Tigers have committed. Not only that, but the cousins and friends of the victims—Bosnian Muslims living elsewhere—will without doubt want revenge, and that means that everyone in X is now in deadly danger of being exterminated by Bosnian Muslims troops. There is only one way for them to protect themselves—to do whatever the Tigers tell them to do, and Arkan and his men will be sure that they are safe from Muslim reprisals. That might, in time, mean more young men from the village will be coming to help with further raids on Bosnian Muslim villages, and to make sure that no one tells on the Tigers, otherwise Arkan and his gang will take their own revenge.

In other words, the poor, hitherto peaceful, members of X are truly sunk, trapped whichever way they look, and with no hope of escape from the violence around them. For in the eyes of all around them, they now share the guilt of their fellow Serbs, even though none of them were terrorists before the fighting began, and even though they wanted nothing more than to live in peace with the Bosnian Muslims.

We can see this on a smaller scale with some real-life examples.

Most accounts of this period show how closely the Serb Orthodox Church worked hand-in-glove with the Serb authorities—most of whom had until recently been supposedly atheistic communists—to scare the daylights out of Serbs beyond the borders of Serbia itself, and, especially of those Serbs living within the borders of Bosnia.

Vamik Volkan describes how many Bosnian Serbs, who had lived peacefully with the local Catholic Croats and Bosnian Muslims, were now persuaded to fear their Islamic neighbors, and how the Bosnian Muslims intended to set up a theocratic regime in which Serbs would be oppressed as they had been in centuries before. Rape and other atrocities now became a means of religious/ethnic defense against the Islamic enemy:

> This fiction led them to increase their own population through raping Bosnian Muslim women. Serbs decided that a child born to a non-Serb woman raped by a Serb would be a Serb and would not carry any vestige of the mother's identity, genetics notwithstanding.

A few brave Serb soldiers protested at having to take part in such hideous genocidal behavior. But they soon found out that they had no option—participation in state-sponsored rape was compulsory, not an optional extra. One such dissenter soon discovered the link between rape and the desire to rid the Balkans of all Muslims:

> The rape is part of it: it spreads fear and terror so that people flee and don't come back. This expulsion and all, it's made the Serbian people in Bosnia into haters, it's sown hatred. The killing and the raping were supposed to teach hate.

It's also no coincidence that the Serbs made heavy use of violent pornography, to desensitize their men and to lower the esteem in which women were held.

All this also ties in with what we have just seen—the whole idea was to commit acts so dreadful that the two peoples—Serb and Bosnian Muslim—could never live near each other ever again, with as many Serbs as possible complicit in creating such circumstances.

As a trained historian, I have always been wary of straying into other academic disciplines. But I do think that Vamik Volkan is able to show, as a psychologist specializing in ethnoreligious conflict, some of the background as to why such terrible things happen, even to ordinary people—we must not forget that most of the atrocities in the Balkan wars in the twentieth century were perpetrated by people who either actually knew each other, as Michael Ignatieff discovered in writing about the 1990s conflict, or by those who at least had been raised not far from where their victims originated.

We should also keep in mind that while, and this is my analogy, the American Civil War was vicious and millions died, the North wanted to beat the South but not to exterminate it. In the carnage we are describing in this chapter, from the Serbian revolt in 1804 down to the Serb massacre of Albanians in Račak in 1999, that the goal was actual physical annihilation of the enemy, the genocide of all Muslims, not just their conquest. No Union general even contemplated something so terrible for even a second, and so when we think of the civil wars in the Balkans we must always remember that something far more terrible was at work than occurred during the War Between the States.

ᐸ 6 ᐳ

A WAR ON TERROR
or, A Case of Continuing Conflict — Life Since 9/11

As A BRITON wearily used to Irish Republican terrorism, it was fascinating—if that is the right expression to use—to be a sympathetic foreigner in America on 9/11. I had just started a new fellowship at the University of Virginia, but had also been injured, coincidentally, just a few days earlier. So I was able to spend two entire days doing nothing but watch the horrific news unfold, as the United States found itself joining so many other countries around the world as a victim of terror.

I was at the appropriately named Institute on Violence, Culture and Survival, and enjoyed a personal link with the nearby Critical Incident Analysis Group (CIAG). The book I was writing on religious terrorism had to be changed immediately to take into account a hitherto little known Islamic extremist group named al Qaeda. All around me, even the experts, such as my friend Professor Larry Adams of the CIAG, a noted scholar both of violent events and of Islam, were in a state of shock. The immunity that the United States had enjoyed from centuries of outside unpleasantness striking its mainland was now over.

I have not normally begun chapters in a personal way, especially since I have dealt with incidents that took place sometimes well over a thousand years ago—even the Crusades began over nine centuries back, however vivid they might seem to some people today. No one we know personally was in them. But 9/11 is something that everyone conscious of that event indelibly remembers, especially if, like me and many friends and pupils of mine, they knew people who were either killed or directly affected on that infamous day.

We all feel, as a result, that the war on terror makes a major personal difference to our own lives—as I write this, my trip home to Britain from my annual teaching semester in the United States is acutely touched by terrorism, since I flew out when it was safe to bring hand luggage onto a plane, and will return with massive restrictions on what I can take back on board. Cambridge, England, where I live, was deeply shaken by Britain's 7/7, since the town is on the direct commuter line into King's Cross, where one of the suicide bombings took place; and my own fifteen-year-old niece was only yards away from the bus explosion as she was a summer intern at the nearby British Museum. Increasingly we all have war stories from the surge in ultraviolent terrorism of recent years.

However, although all around me in Charlottesville, Virginia, were in an entirely understandable state of shock and disbelief in the days following 9/11, I found myself compelled to agree with the distinguished Oxford and Yale military historian Sir Michael Howard that the world, despite the scale of events in New York and Washington DC, did *not* change on 9/11. Rather (and I am adding my own interpretation here), what happened was that, tragically, America found itself caught up in a conflict that has lasted for over a thousand years, and which has a strong likelihood of remaining around for a long time to come. What took place was that the United States, hitherto insulated from such horrors by distance and geography, found itself part of the fray, and lost the immunity it had enjoyed since settlers first came over four hundred years ago.

For everywhere else in the world, religious terrorism has resurrected itself with a terrible vengeance, especially since the

end of the cold war. In fact there is almost, in some circles today, a sense of nostalgia for the old cold war certainties, with
two supposedly equal superpowers, between them both in conflict and, at the same time, able to ensure that no local squabble
ever escalated so far that thermonuclear war erupted and wiped
out the planet. (As someone who had numerous dissident
friends behind the Iron Curtain prior to 1989, I do not share
such a nostalgic view of 1945–91, but alas it is true that the
world is now a considerably more fissile and unstable place
than it was during those years.)

Much nonsense was written during post-1991 conflicts in
places such as the Balkans (an area upon which I have written
two books) about so-called "ancient conflicts," as if, for example, Serbs and Bosnians have spent centuries killing each other,
and the mass murders in the 1990s were just another episode in
an age-old saga. In fact, many of the religious warfare issues
discussed in this book were and are more complex than that.

And yet, although the actual conflicts might be new—no
country such as Yugoslavia existed prior to 1918, for instance,
and in 2006 even the vestigial remains vanished from the map—
I think that the *basic* causes have been the same for well over a
thousand years, even if the name of the participants changes.

In other words, what we saw reemerge after the end of the
cold war in 1991 and what hit America with such hideous force
on 9/11, is in reality no different from what captured Jerusalem
in both 638 and 1099: conflict in the name of a religious faith.
This is why so many have been slaughtered in centuries past,
and why nearly 8,000 were murdered in Srebrenica in 1995 and
over 3,000 in Washington, DC, and New York in September
2001.

What is different, however, is that the largest and most
powerful early twenty-first-century power, the United States, is
directly involved for the first time in a conflict the kind of
which the rest of humanity has been suffering since time immemorial.

The world did not change on 9/11: what altered was that Americans now understand through their nation's own experience, and maybe directly in their own lives, what religious violence is all about.

This is, of course, despite the fact that the overwhelming majority of Americans, whether themselves deeply religious or secular, do not see it as a conflict between Christianity and Islam. This is, indeed, part of the problem, since most Westerners separate church and state, and find it near impossible to understand the mentality of those who do not make that now centuries-old distinction. In Islam, on the other hand, the fusion of church/faith and state is integral to the very nature of their religious outlook.

(To make the last personal reference in this chapter, Muslims to whom I have spoken in off the record consultations are fascinated to meet a white Westerner who is himself actively religious—the fact that I am a practicing Christian, far from antagonizing them, usually results in a sense of relief on their part: thank goodness for meeting someone who actually understands, as do both believing Muslims and Christians, what religious faith is all about. While they know, therefore, that I do not share their Islamic beliefs, they also grasp that I am, in one sense, more like them as a person of faith, in what has become an increasingly secular, irreligious world. I should add, though, that these are all non-violent Muslims to whom I have spoken, often brave people keen for interreligious harmony and good neighborly relations. What an active terrorist would do on meeting me is thankfully something I have yet to discover. . . .)

The resurrection of religion as a major player in world affairs, not just in terms of violence and terrorism but also in many other respects as well, has caught the secular academic world completely off guard. The secularization theory of Harvard specialist Harvey Cox presumed that, as time progressed, most people globally would get less religious rather than more devout. Perhaps because so many Western universities are bas-tions of secularism, not by any means necessarily in a hostile sense, the resurgence of religion as the twentieth century progressed came as a major shock.

Fortunately, not all academics were ignorant of life beyond the Western campus. We ought to consider what experts have written about in recent years, since the authors help to put mystifying events into a helpful framework. I should add that the synthesis in what follows is my own but, alas, as some of the works that follow are academic, they may not be known to a wider audience.

University of California sociologist Mark Juergensmeyer wrote two highly influential books on religious violence. The first, called *The New Cold War? Religious Nationalism Confronts the Secular State,* came out as early as 1993, and his major seller *Terror in the Mind of God* managed to have Osama bin Laden on the front cover and be published long *before* 9/11. Similarly, the French specialist on Islam and Islamic extremism, Gilles Kepel, wrote his *The Revenge of God* long before the present wave of international religious terrorism, which he can therefore be said to have predicted, and which has, along with Juergensmeyer's books, been vindicated by subsequent events.

Then, in terms of understanding the global reach of the religious revival, looking in this instance mainly at its nonviolent forms, Philip Jenkins's book *The Next Christendom* demonstrates that Christianity is no longer a Western-based religion but has returned to its Two-Thirds World roots (There are seventeen times as many *active* Episcopalians in Nigeria, for instance, than in England, that denomination's country of origin.) Jenkins does mention, though, that while in some parts of the world, such as in Latin America, Christianity's growth does not involve violent conflict, in many other regions it does—especially where, in West Africa and Southeast Asia, for example, it is coming up against an equally missionary-orientated and also growing global faith, Islam.

This brings us to the final set of background ideas to consider before we launch into a detailed look at the current war on terror and whether it really is what it outwardly seems to be.

Here there are two quite distinct theories, one almost infamous and one probably little known outside academia. Both precede 9/11, and many media pundits declared it to be fully vindicated by that day's events. The second has remained in comparative obscurity, yet, to me, is a much better understanding of what the current wave of religious terrorism is all about than the more famous and controversial thesis.

The first is the *clash of civilizations* theory of Professor Samuel Huntington of Harvard University, first put before a mainly academic audience in the journal *Foreign Affairs* in 1993 and then, after that article swiftly gained international notoriety well beyond university circles, in a major best-selling book of 1996, *The Clash of Civilizations and the Remaking of World Order*. The second is by Bassam Tibi, a Muslim professor teaching in Germany, whose book for the University of California Press entitled *The Challenge of Fundamentalism: Political Islam and the New World Disorder* came out in 1998, followed by a post-9/11 paperback edition in 2002.

Huntington, in his notorious article and book, said that in future, now that the cold war was over, future conflicts would be based upon what he called "civilizations," each civilization being based upon what different groups of people shared in common with one another in particular parts of the world. To him, the highest common factor points of unity were based in essence upon shared culture and religious heritage. For this reason, he named the individual civilization groups by religion, and this is where his ideas became controversial.

Whatever our actual faith, we in the West live in the Western Christian region, based upon Protestant and Catholic versions of Christianity combined—as he explained in depth (and as I have written elsewhere on this subject), both these brands of the faith have the Reformation in common, in that Catholicism had to respond to the changes that Protestantism introduced. In addition, Western Europe, and its American daughter culture, also had enjoyed the effects of the Renaissance in the fifteenth century and the Enlightenment in the eighteenth.

Reformation and Renaissance were two seismic events in history and thought that passed by the other Christian civilization, the Orthodox, centered upon Russia, although historically Orthodoxy had originally, as we saw, been based upon the Byzantine culture and empire. In addition, Orthodoxy had suffered under religiously alien Islamic rule, disposed of earlier in Russia's case, but not until the early twentieth century in parts of the Balkans. Only Hungary, in Western Christianity, had undergone such a fate, and in that case comparatively briefly.

Other civilizations are somewhat self-explanatory — Hindu centered around India, Shinto around Japan, and Confucian around China, and Buddhist in Southeast Asia.

But what made the Huntington thesis truly controversial was his description of Islamic civilization, and, in particular, his appellation of it as having "bloody borders." In other words, he seemed to be saying, where you have Islam you have sanguinary conflicts, and violence.

On 9/11, many in the press therefore saw that event — one perpetrated by Muslims in the name of Islam — as the "Huntington moment," that the theory was indeed true and that events had come to pass that confirmed what Huntington had predicted eight years before.

Huntington had in fact gained the phrase "the clash of civilizations" from an article on Islam by Bernard Lewis, the doyen of Middle Eastern studies in the United States, in an article entitled "The Roots of Muslim Rage," in the monthly *Atlantic*, as far back as 1990.

But while, as we saw looking at the fallout of 1918, many Muslims, violent and peaceful alike, have indeed had a strong

sense of rage at what they perceived to be their humiliation at
the hands of the West after the fall of the Ottoman Empire,
Lewis in his own article showed clearly that it was not as simple as that. In the past few years, one of the main cheerleaders
for the invasion of Iraq has been Lewis, and the reason he has
given in print (and in person to me when we met in 2005) is
that Iraq has a large educated middle class, including many
professional women, and that it is therefore capable of democracy and freedom in the Western sense of those terms. Even
back in 1990, Lewis felt that a permanent sense of clash was not
inevitable, and I think that is what has fueled his optimism ever
since.

This is not the place to say whether the rosy Lewis view of
a "liberated" Iraq—and thus the invasion of that country in
2003—is and was justified. But it is, I think, important to say
that the inventor of the term "the clash of civilizations" does not
have anything like as rigid a view as the professor who has
made the phrase famous, Samuel Huntington.

Another Harvard professor, David Little, spoke to me in
2001 (and wrote for the U.S. Institute of Peace) about a "con-
fusion of civilizations." Little, along with many others, sees a
battle taking place *within* Islam. When I was writing this chapter, in the summer of 2006, I read in a single newspaper report
of well over twenty Shiite Muslims in Iraq having been slaughtered by extremist Sunni Muslims.

In fact *most* of the killing in Iraq after the Western invasion
has not been Iraqis killing British and American troops—
although U.S. casualties of all kinds have not been small—but
of Shiite Muslims being killed by (and in some cases killing in
retaliation) Sunni Muslims, either from within Iraq, or, in the
case of al-Zarqawi, the now-dead Jordanian-born guerrilla
leader, Sunnis from other parts of the Middle East. (Pakistan
has also seen much Sunni/Shiite killing.)

What is it that the extremists believe? We have all heard of

Osama bin Laden and al Qaeda, an organization that many think is now best seen not as a single malign group but rather as a franchise of like-minded fanatics, who often have, at best, tenuous direct links with one another but shared religious views and outlook.

Conclusion

Our look at religious warfare has spanned a period more than fourteen hundred years long. We have seen small tribes create vast empires, with results that remain with us in the twenty-first century. We have observed how neighbor kills neighbor, if the cause appears cosmically sanctioned by God. We have come to the sad conclusion that the age of religious warfare is with us still, as potent a force as it has always been, throughout history.

We have also seen, I trust, that religious warfare is not limited to any particular faith—in that respect we are all guilty. While it may be convenient for some to attach unique blame to one faith or another, I think we have learned enough to say that to do so would be unfair. At the moment it might well appear that, for example, Islam is the guilty party, with Islamic terrorists spewing forth hatred in the name of the Muslim faith, and with innocent Westerners their main victims. But in the recent past Muslims have been victims as well as perpetrators, the eight thousand dead of Srebrenica still crying out to us of their complete innocence. Muslims and Christians alike fall prey to rampaging extremist Hindu mobs in India, who want to have a subcontinent rid of unbelievers in a way no different from the extremist Muslim wish to have an entirely infidel free Arabian Peninsula. The religion is different in each case, but the exclusivist demands are the same.

It is always good to end on a note of optimism. I wish! A

few years ago I did just that in a book on a related topic, with pious hopes that Iran, a country in which many of the young people were actively pro-Western, and which had a reformist president, would slowly get better and better, with wonderful consequences for peace, and what president Khatami expressed as a "dialogue of civilizations." But how wrong all our hopes proved to be, with Iran even more in the extremist camp than ever before, and with a leader whom even some of the religious hierarchy are realizing is a dangerous fanatic, possibly soon armed with a nuclear arsenal that can threaten global as well as regional stability.

But then we also saw how no one predicted—perhaps with the rare exceptions of Emmanuel Todd and Daniel Patrick Moynihan—the peaceful end of the cold war, the demise not just of the Soviet bloc but also of the USSR itself, and a liberated Central and Eastern Europe rapidly joining the community of free and prosperous nations. The nuclear Armageddon that so terrified generations of us in the 1950s through to the 1980s never happened, and even though prospects for pluralist democracy in Russia do not look great, World War III and global annihilation seem more than unlikely.

War is always changing, and as we enter the twenty-first century, it is doing so again. We now have what the experts call *asymmetric* warfare—the kind that British and American troops are discovering, to their cost, in places such as Iraq and Afghanistan, and which the terrorist acts of 9/11 are also a classic example.

At the moment, Islam is involved in both, but that could, I suspect, be a passing stage—no one in 1980, for example, when Tito was still alive and ruling Yugoslavia, imagined that within fifteen years of his death the worst carnage in Europe since World War II would be seen in the Balkans, and that atrocities unseen since the Nazi era would once again be taking place, this time not in the name of race but of religion. So while the examples that follow both include Islam, we should not presume that that will continue to be the case, since, to use one of Donald Rumsfeld's infamous phrases, there are plenty of "unknown unknowns" out there as well as the "known unknowns" that might be likely to happen!

Asymmetric warfare is, I would argue, not as new as the military experts say it is. If, for example, one thinks again of Balkan history, there is little doubt that Tito's Partisan forces, admittedly with plenty of Western aid, were able to tie down German forces that were considerably out of proportion to the number of Partisan troops that they were aiming, and failing, to suppress. There has actually been a name for this for over two hundred years, one invented in the Spanish struggle against Napoleon's forces in the early nineteenth-century Peninsula War. The Spaniards called their resistance fighters *guerrillas*, and if one looks at what is happening in Iraq and Afghanistan, there is, to me, no real difference between Napoleonic Spain, Second World War Yugoslavia, and twenty-first-century Afghanistan. If I am right, then *this* part of asymmetric warfare is just a new name for an old phenomenon.

However, there is a sense in which the pundits are right, and we *are* witnessing something entirely new, and therefore very dangerous for a West that has traditionally been taught to fight a very different kind of war.

For centuries, wars apart from civil ones have been between nation states. This is what is called the Westphalian system, after the Treaty of Westphalia signed in 1648 that we observed in an earlier chapter that ended Europe's last religious war. Our armies are trained and equipped to fight wars between one country and another. If World War III had occurred, with the cold war becoming nuclear hot, that would still have been the case: a war between the states of NATO and those in the Warsaw Pact. It is, in fact, for precisely such a war that our armies are designed.

Of recent wars, those in Kosovo and in the first Gulf War both fell into the traditional pattern. NATO countries attacked Serbia, to liberate Kosovo, and a coalition of nation states in 1991 attacked Iraq so as to free Kuwait.

However, what was going on during that time in Afghanistan, and in the years following, should have alerted us to a new kind of warfare, not between states, but between rival protagonists holding different views of the world. In Afghanistan we helped the Islamic guerrilla forces, the mujahideen, to get rid of the Soviets. But we then forgot about that region, greatly to our own detriment. Because our cold war enemy—the USSR—had been vanquished, as much with Western military equipment as by brave Afghan fighters, we then paid no more attention to what was happening. This, as many books since (especially those by Chalmers Johnson, such as *Blowback*) demonstrated clearly, was a massive mistake and led very directly to 9/11.

For the fighting did not stop when the last Soviet troops left—in some ways, that is when the *real* war began. One bunch of thuggish warlords battled with another for control of the country, and in the end they were defeated by an enemy far worse than any of them, the Taliban, and their Arab allies, Osama bin Laden among them.

This, I would argue, was something new.

The old Westphalian system, that dated back to the treaty of Westphalia that ended the Thirty Years' War in 1648, was about controlling a particular state, and for reasons of state— to make your state bigger or more powerful, or less likely to be attacked, or for all sorts of other, state-related, reasons. Even Nazism, although it was a racist ideology, fits into this pattern, as the goal of the Nazis was to make Germany, a state, into the most powerful on earth.

Now it is true that the initial goal of the Taliban was to take over control of a state, in this case Afghanistan. But although most Taliban are also members of a particular tribal group—the

Pashtun, who also live in large numbers in Pakistan—national or tribal domination was not their ultimate goal. For the main thing about the Taliban, who swiftly took control of the bulk of the country, was not their ethnicity but their *religion*.

There was a religious nationalist element in, for example, Serbian behavior toward the Croats and Bosnian Muslims. So religious warfare in and of itself was not new to the twentieth century. But in that the Serbs were nationalists, out to create a Greater Serbia, theirs was both a religious conflict and a straight nationalist one, at the same time.

However, if we look at Afghanistan under the Taliban, it is clear that theirs was not a Pashtun nationalist movement. For example, the Northern Alliance in that conflict was heavily based on the Tajik minority to the north. Many of the warriors, and a considerable amount of their money, were from non-Pashtuns, from the so-called Afghan Arabs of whom Osama bin Laden and his al Qaeda network were simply the most famous.

In other words, we have moved from a classic Westphalian nation state–based system of conflict to one in which national borders are incidental—a war based not on the country you live in but upon the religious beliefs that you hold. Yes, al Qaeda was based in a nation state—Afghanistan—but that was as much an address of convenience as anything else. The aim of the Taliban and their al Qaeda allies was not to create a Greater Afghanistan, but to resurrect the Islamic caliphate, an empire that as we saw, was not based on nationality but upon a religious concept.

Much academic ink has been spilled on whether al Qaeda, and its ideology, is in fact modern while using ancient pre-modern concepts, such as the caliphate; or whether it really is a return to an altogether different, earlier, system of thought based on entirely preenlightenment values, and upon a solely religious interpretation of the world in which we live, even though al Qaeda does not hesitate to use modern technology, such as airplanes and videocassettes, to execute and spread their message.

I tend more to the latter view, while at the same time feeling that there is nothing incompatible with a religious outlook on life and acceptance of all the good things that modern technology has brought us. But that, however, is not the main argument here.

The key point, I think, is that we do now have a non-Westphalian concept of war. The attack of 9/11 was not, in the traditional sense, an attack *by the country of Afghanistan on the country of the United States*. The attacks were planned in Afghanistan, and they took place in New York and Washington, DC. But it was not a country vs. country conflict, even though it ended up like that when Western troops landed in Afghanistan and got rid of the Taliban government. Rather, so far as the predominantly Saudi Arabian perpetrators were concerned, it was part of the ongoing conflict between Islam and its enemies, between the faithful of the Dar al-Islam and a land that embodied the Dar al-Harb. Subsequent attacks in Spain and Britain have shown this—it is the West that is the terrorists' enemy, not any particular country as such within it.

Countless commentators noted then and since that in terms of the costs there was no proportion at all between what it cost the attackers and the damage that they did to their target. Some hotel bills, a few airline tickets, and the purchase of box cutters are completely asymmetric to the devastation caused and of the massive expense that the war on terror has cost Western governments since 2001.

Under the old system, when one side conquered its enemy, that was it! The war was won and over. When the Allies beat the Nazis in 1945, the Second World War in Europe was finished.

But under asymmetric warfare, how do you declare victory? Afghanistan was conquered, the Taliban beaten, al Qaeda forced into hiding (and some of its leaders captured) — and yet the war on terror continues, now in places where it had not existed before, such as Indonesia, with its atrocities against Western tourists, London on 7/7, and above all in Iraq, which for all intents and purposes has replaced Afghanistan as the ideal training ground for jihadist guerrillas to fight the West. Massive U.S. firepower enabled Iraq to be conquered remarkably quickly in 2003, and with hardly any Western casualites. But now, as I write this, the whole strategy seems rapidly to be coming unstuck, not because of pitched tank battles between American and Iraqi forces — the old way — but because of asymmetric warfare, with many of the enemy not Iraqi nationalists but Muslim warriors from all sorts of Islamic countries fighting what they believe to be a jihad, a holy war. Not only that, but it is also clear that the Taliban are back in force in Afghanistan, and that Western forces there are having a terrible time trying to keep that country from imploding all over again.

This neatly takes us to the other, also new, kind of asymmetric war — one waged not with national borders, but in people's minds. Here traditional armies are useless, something that should have been obvious to the West, since we essentially won the cold war not through NATO forces but by winning the altogether nonmilitary battle of ideas. It was the concept of freedom, those of liberty and democracy, and the desire for human rights that prevailed in 1989, and without a Western shot being fired.

As I write this, a furious debate is happening in Britain between the wider English community and the growing Muslim minority, and also, in parallel, within the Islamic population itself. The touchstone issue is whether or not Muslim women should wear the full *niqab*, which covers the face and renders it invisible, or just the *hijab*, which is not much different from a Western scarf, and leaves the face completely visible. Behind all this, certainly so far as the Muslim community is concerned, is: what is legitimate to wear that simultaneously enables us to be devout followers of Islam, and yet at the same time recognizes that, because we live in a predominantly non-Muslim culture, we should make some kind of accommodation to the majority in whose presence we live: how can I be both a loyal Muslim and a patriotic Briton at the same time?

Britain—and, I would suspect, the USA—is keen for its Islamic citizens not to be forced to make a choice between religion and citizenship, that it really should be possible to be a loyal British citizen and also an actively practicing Muslim. In France, for example, this is becoming harder, since Muslim girls cannot even wear the *hijab* at school, as that is deemed incompatible with the French concept of the secular (literally, layman) state, *laïcité*.

All this might seem just culture wars under another guise. But to see it as that would, I feel, be highly misleading and also dangerous. We are not here talking of political correctness or any of the other issues that so agitate people on both sides of the Atlantic. What we are really looking at here is how best for Westerners such as most of us to help the right side win the current ideological battle that is being waged, the internal struggle for the soul and future direction of Islam itself.

In the cold war, some of us, perhaps in a foolhardy way, did our best to help dissidents behind the Iron Curtain. I remember scary trips to see friends in places such as Prague or Budapest, to help those who wanted freely to exercise their rights as religious believers to practice their faith.

Some friends of mine thought that the best way to help was to smuggle in literature from the West. I thought this was a mistake, and so did my Czech and Hungarian friends. Their reason was interesting: Western-smuggled literature linked the dissidents to the political enemies of the countries in which they were living—it linked my friends specifically to NATO and the West. They far preferred to print their own clandestine literature. Freedom was not a Western concept, but a universal human right, one to which they were entitled as humans, regardless of whether those of us in the West supported such rights—which we did—or not.

I feel the same struggle is happening within Islam today: what direction should be taken by those in the wholly new situation for Muslims, namely that of being a minority of the faithful in the land of infidels, the West. Are they brave members of the Islamic *umma*, living among the infidels, or are they, as moderate Muslims would hope, dwelling with fellow humans in a land of peace: a Dar al-Salaam. (To some Muslims there is another option—the Dar al-Sulh, or land of truce, but for many that ceased to be an option after numerous Western countries joined America in invading Iraq in 2003.)

Some pessimists, such as the Egyptian writer Ba't Yeor, see Europe swiftly becoming "Eurabia," a view held by some of the more hard-line neoconservatives in the United States. They view the way in which Western liberal inclined governments give in to Islam on the grounds of political correctness as a sign of surrender, and they extrapolate dire figures from the birthrate of Muslim women to end up with an Islamic majority in Europe in a few years' time.

To me, this is all alarmist nonsense. What is interesting, as Penn State University religious expert Philip Jenkins writes in his influential *The Next Christendom*, is that in many parts of Europe *Christianity* is, in fact, on the increase, and in greater numbers than Islam. Jenkins is an interesting commentator in that, being British, and at a secular state university, he is not seen as part of the culture wars within the United States in the way that other experts, such as Peter Berger of Boston, are perceived as being politically and culturally prejudiced by many in the media and academia. Anyone who writes a book for Oxford University Press, and then appears on Pat Robertson's television station to comment on the same subject, has achieved a rare feat!

But I also think that Jenkins is right. If one looks at London, to take one European city that has suffered from terrorism and contains within its very large Islamic population a proven core of Muslim terrorists, one would think that the doom-mongers are right. However, London is also one of the parts of Britain in which traditional Christianity is also growing, con-trary to most trends in the rest of Europe. Not only that, but as both Jenkins and respected British statisticians have shown, over half the active church-going Christians in London are black, of African origin. One of London's largest churches, Kingsway International, has a Nigerian pastor, and the capital (and some other parts of Britain) now have missionaries from Nigeria, Peru, Korea, and other parts of the Two-Thirds World coming to evangelize the post-Christian secular Britons. For every white Briton who turns to Islam, there is probably a sim-ilar white English person converted to Christianity by an African or Asian missionary.

For as Jenkins and other academics have now realized — something that many of the rest of us have known since a ma-jor international congress in Lausanne in 1974 — Christianity is now an overwhelmingly nonwhite religion: Jenkins quotes the truism that many Two-Thirds World leaders have been telling us for over thirty years, that within a few decades only 20 per-cent of Christians will be whites of European descent.

One of the myths propagated by (and, to be fair, genuinely believed in) by al Qaeda and extremist Muslims of all types is that Christianity is both the enemy of Islam and also the reli-gion of the West, something we saw in the statements by bin Laden after 9/11. But statistically this will soon be completely false, if it has not already been so for many years, if not decades, already. Most practicing Christians in the world today live outside the West, indeed outside the United States.

According to CIA/U.S. government statistics, there are now 100 *million* active Christians today in the People's Repub-lic of China alone. (Jenkins estimates there are between 50 and 80 million, most experts I know would put the figure at 80 million, but because the vast majority of Chinese Christians attend "underground" unofficial and illegal churches outside the government-sanctioned Three-Self Patriotic Churches, it is hard to tell—the CIA figures might be right.) However many there really are—and even the lower estimates of 80 million are still incredibly high, when one thinks that there were 2 million Chinese Christians when Western missionaries were expelled in 1951—it is clear that there are far more Christians in China than in most other countries in the world today.

Similarly, while there are notionally 25 million baptized members of the Church of England in Britain, no more than 1 million, or 4 percent, of those ever attend any kind of church even as much as once a year. But in Nigeria, there are now 20 million *active* Anglicans, who regularly attend church every Sunday, which means that now, more than forty years after Nigerian independence, the Church of England in Nigeria has twenty times as many *practicing* adherents than does the mother church back in Britain.

In other words, Christianity is reverting to its Two-Thirds World roots, a faith primarily of non-Western people. Islam has never been a Western faith in any sense, and so the two major universal evangelizing religions are now meeting head-on in competition for converts in many parts of the world, and in the twenty-first century without any reference at all to the West. It is Nigerian Christians competing for souls with Nigerian Muslims, Indonesian Muslims the same with Indonesian Christians, and a similar story in many other parts of the developing world.

It is here, I think, that the real competition will come, and is already doing so with considerable amounts of bloodshed already, as the two missionary faiths clash with each other in areas that are, spiritually speaking, up for grabs. As Paul Marshall, the leading British-American expert connected to Freedom House, once told me, we may not often read of such clashes in our newspapers or see it on our television screens, but thou-

sands of people have been killed in recent years in violence between Muslims and Christians, in Nigeria and Indonesia in
particular, but on a lesser scale in other regions as well.

Here one must be fair—in a place such as India, it is the
Christians and Muslims who are the victims not the perpetrators, with extremist Hindu mobs putting both groups to death,
burning both churches and mosques, and often with the con-
nivance of politicians and police linked to Hindu nationalist
parties. But it is also true to say that Hindu mobs do not kill
people in Britain, where there is a large Hindu and Muslim
population, nor do Hindus take their violence outside of India
itself—there has been no Hindu equivalent of 9/11. Where the
conflict might be horrendously dangerous is if India and Pakistan, both of whom have large numbers of nuclear weapons,
ever go to war with each other, and the conflict escalates into
nuclear war.

It is reckoned, from research undertaken in 2002, that up to
58 million people would be killed in an Indo-Pakistani nuclear
exchange—and that is to exclude those who *might* die in other
countries if the wind blew strongly in one direction (toward
Iran and Israel) or the other (toward China and Thailand).
Since Pakistan exists solely because of religious differences—
many Pakistanis, including President Musharraf, were born in
India, and emigrated there after 1947—this would not only be
the first-ever nuclear war between two countries, but a religious war as well, since many of the guerrilla groups operating
in Kashmir, the province that is disputed between the two
countries, are Islamic in nature and composition, and have
close links with al Qaeda as well as, so many assert, with the
Pakistani military and intelligence services.

But I think that an Indo-Pakistani conflict would be the
only one to fit into the old Westphalian system, of a war between two nation-states, even if, as in the case of India and
Pakistan, the war would be a religious one, between a Muslim

country and one that has an increasingly desecularized Hindu identity.

To me, other conflicts would fit more into the post-Westphalian pattern, either of the kind of asymmetric warfare that we are seeing in Iraq, or perhaps within nation states, with different factions in each fighting each other.

I would argue, we are actually seeing this in Iraq as I write this, with the predominant casualties not being American or British occupying armies, but one group of Iraqis, the Sunni, fighting another, the Shia. Since the great battle of Karbala in 680 took place in what is now Iraq, we are seeing the next phase in what is, one could legitimately here contend, a genuinely ancient struggle, between two strands of Islam. For more than thirteen hundred years, under the rule of the Ummayads, then the Abbasids, and then the centuries of Ottoman dominance, the Shia of the region outside of Iran were a repressed people, but now, because of the overthrow of the Sunni group around Saddam Hussein in 2003, a majority at last. (A point to remember—we are talking here of Arab vs. Arab, since the Kurds, while ethnically different, are also Sunni.) Not since the seventh century have the Shia Arab Muslims been able to rule in their own heartland—the various Shia dynasties that exercised power under the later, weak Sunni Arab Abbasid caliphs were from Iran or were ethnic Turks—and now is a thirteen-hundred-years-plus payback time.

Likewise, the conflict between Christian and Muslim in nations such as Nigeria and Indonesia is within a nation state, especially, in the former case, for the middle region, in which neither Christians nor Muslims currently prevail, but in which both faiths are actively winning converts.

Such, too, might be the conflict, if assimilation goes the wrong way, in Europe, with the Muslim minority there uncertain of how far to go in identifying with the host countries. Muslims wishing to become citizens of the Netherlands have to look at movies of gay couples and seminaked women on a beach, to see if they are culturally able to become citizens of a pluralist and increasingly highly secular society. This might seem strange to the rest of us, but there has been murder and violence in the Netherlands, and the legendary Dutch tolerance — often seen in matters sexual or drug-related — is now becoming something very much in the past.

In all of Europe, even if most Muslims do assimilate in one form or another, either actively, or in terms of grudging toleration of their surroundings, it only takes a tiny minority to be violent, and to take up terrorism, and thereby to create chaos and community disharmony completely out of all proportion to their numbers. This, of course, creates a vicious cycle, since anger by the Western majority to the Muslim minority after extremist acts, in which innocent Muslims are tarred with the terrorist brush in a white backlash, only increases the sense of Islamic community paranoia and thereby greatly helps the genuine extremists in winning converts to the cause.

That is why I tend to feel that if Muslim women sincerely want to wear the full veil, the *niqab*, we should let them, as it does no harm and shows the Islamic community that they can keep their religious practices and live peacefully as full citizens within the majority Western community.

(I say "Western" deliberately, as no country in Europe even approaches the level of practicing Christians that exist in the United States today. Here I agree fully with Boston sociologist of religion Peter Berger that while America disproves secularization theory, since it remains profoundly religious, Europe is profoundly secular, even if my British fellow Christians still wish to maintain that the United Kingdom is a legally Christian country. It may be in theory, but those of us who actually attend church are a tiny minority, and there may soon be more attending a mosque on Fridays than go regularly to a church on Sundays.)

But this is very different from appeasement, which never worked in history in the past, and does not do so today in any context, either. What applies to one faith should to another — as I write this two public service employees were disciplined for wearing a small Christian cross at work. In one case, she was able to continue wearing one, so long as she chose one that was smaller than her original model, and with the second case, the verdict is still awaited. The idea that different faiths should no longer be able to proselytize, in case another faith is upset, does seem to take political correctness too far. In the West, we should instead argue that all faiths have the right to evangelize, Christians, Muslims, Hindus, and the like, and that Muslim countries ought to allow similar freedom in their countries, rather than their present practice, which is sometimes to go as far as executing any of their citizens who convert to another faith.

As I mentioned earlier, no one but a very few would, even in early 1989, have predicted the fall of the Soviet bloc later that year and the dispossession of the USSR itself in 1991. So what will happen in terms of religious conflict in the future is equally difficult to predict. But I think it likely that such clashes will continue, and do so mainly in terms of the post-Westphalian, asymmetric kind we have just seen.

It is possible that a nuclear Iran might want to start a war, but since an Iran-Israel conflict could swiftly escalate into a nuclear one, other powers, including those currently staying out such as China and Russia, would want to intervene to stop it, especially as fallout radiation might cross into Russian or Chinese territory. Similarly, it would take a very fanatical BJP (Bharatiya Janata Party) Hindu nationalist government, or the fall of Pakistan into extremist Muslim hands, for a major-scale nuclear war between those two countries to break out, with, as we saw, potentially tens of millions of casualties.

But precisely because such awful results would happen

from such nuclear carnage, I tend to think that that is why such doomsday conflicts will not happen, although I could be proved horrifically wrong.

However, even if nuclear annihilation may not take place, that does not mean that thousands will no longer die in religious clashes around the world—far from it.

Here we need to consider the Hinsley thesis, invented by Second World War cryptanalyst and code-breaker, and later historian, Sir Harry Hinsley. Hinsley, later a British guru on international relations, had, during the cold war, a theory that in fact cheered many of us up. The Hinsley notion was that so terrible are the results of nuclear war—especially if it led to the so-called "nuclear winter" that would result from all the dust contaminating the ozone layer such that life on earth became impossible because the sun's rays would be shut out—that both sides knew that such a war could never be won. So nuclear weapons, paradoxically, ensure that nuclear war never happens—and, indeed, any kind of war between the USA and the USSR and their respective allies never happened during the tense cold war. Deterrence worked.

But if total annihilation—which is what nuclear weapons would have ensured, or Mutually Assured Destruction (MAD!)— (was *not* likely, then neither was war. This is exactly what we have seen since the end of the cold war in 1991: lots more war, hundreds of thousands, if not by now millions of people, mainly civilians, all killed and usually, as in places far afield as Rwanda and Bosnia, in peculiarly gruesome circumstances. Not only that, but, if one takes the last two mentioned conflicts, in Africa and the Balkans, these have also been primarily civil wars, internal sets of massacres, with weapons as simple as machetes, in the case of Rwanda, being used to slaughter tens of thousands of innocent civilians, the victims often being well known to their killers. Precisely because the world will *not* come to an end—as would have happened in a nuclear World War III—war is more likely to happen and thousands of people die as a result. It is the absence of Armageddon that has brought war back war into our midst, and thus posed a massively higher threat to ordinary people — as we saw on 9/11 and 7/7 — than existed in the cold war.

This is, I would argue, much more than a simple "war on terrorism," since it is not terrorists in the al Qaeda sense that are killing their neighbors in places such as central Nigeria or the various islands of Indonesia where religious conflict is taking place. Of course, terrorism is part of such a wider clash, especially that of "universalisms" between an actively expanding/evangelizing Islam with an equally multinational/cross-cultural Christianity, as we saw earlier when looking at Bassam Tibi's convincing theory. But so, too, are the local conflicts in Two-Thirds World countries that hardly ever make their way into newspapers in the West: they are equally religious conflicts, even though terrorism in the 9/11, anti-Western, antiglobalization sense is not present. A Nigerian murdered by childhood contemporaries is as much a victim as an American in the Pentagon or Twin Towers: the style of death might be dissimilar, but the cause, religious violence, is the same.

So, pleasant though it would be, ending on a note of optimism might be a hard thing to do. Naturally it would be great to be proved wrong, by an outbreak of religious peace, tolerance and understanding that prevails over the violence we have seen not just in recent years but also in the fourteen-hundred-year time span of this book. But somehow I cannot see human nature changing that suddenly! Religious conflict, the turning of faiths supposedly based upon peace into cosmic endorsed violence, will not, if we are realistic, ever go away. It is, as my editor said, the dark heart of humanity, the desire to kill one's fellow creatures, and do so with the sanction of the divine.

Bibliography

Note: Inclusion in this bibliography simply means that I used the book—given the controversial nature of much of the subject matter, inclusion does *not* imply agreement. What follows is a selection of the numerous books read—and if I had included all the articles, the bibliography would have been three or four times as long. Special thanks are due to the Boatwright Library of the University of Richmond in Richmond, Virginia, for finding so many of these books.

Abdullah, Thabit. *A Short History of Iraq.* London and Harlow: Pearson Longman, 2003.

Adelson, Roger. *London and the Invention of the Middle East.* New Haven, CT: Yale University Press, 1996.

Ahmed, Akbar. *Islam Under Siege.* Cambridge, UK: Polity Press, 2003.

———. *Islam Today: A Short Introduction to the Muslim World.* London: I.B. Tauris, 1999.

———, and Brian Forst (eds.). *After Terror.* Cambridge, UK: Polity Press, 2005.

Akbar, M. J. *Shade of Swords: Jihad and the Conflict Between Islam and Christianity.* London: Routledge, 2002.

Allen, S. J., and Emilie Amt, *The Crusades: A Reader.* Peterborough, Ontario: Broadview Press, 2003.

Armstrong, Karen. *A History of God.* New York: Ballantine, 1993.

————. *Islam: A Short History*. London: Weidenfeld and Nicolson, 2000.

————. *Muhammad: A Biography of the Prophet*. London: Phoenix, 2001.

Asher, Michael. *Lawrence: The Uncrowned King of Arabia*. London: Viking, 1998.

Ayoub, Mahmoud. *The Crisis of Muslim History: Religion and Politics in Early Islam*. Oxford: Oneworld Publications, 2003.

————. *Islam: Faith and History*. Oxford: Oneworld Publications, 2004.

Bachrach, David S. *Religion and the Conduct of War*. Woodbridge: Boydell Press, 2003.

Bard, Mitchell. *The Complete Idiot's Guide to the Middle East Conflict* (2nd ed.). New York: Pearson Education, 2003.

Benjamin, Daniel, and Steven Simon. *The Age of Sacred Terror*. New York: Random House, 2002.

Bergen, Peter. *Holy War Inc*. London: Weidenfeld and Nicolson, 2001.

Bloom, Jonathan, and Sheila Blair. *Islam: A Thousand Years of Faith and Power*. New Haven, CT: Yale University Press, 2002.

Bloom, Mia. *Dying to Kill: The Allure of Suicide Terror*. New York: Columbia University Press, 2005.

Bonney, Richard. *Jihad: From Qur'an to bin Laden*. Basingstoke: Palgrave, 2004.

Bostom, Andrew (ed.). *The Legacy of Jihad*. Amherst, NY: Prometheus Books, 2005.

Bregman, Ahron, and Jihan El-Tahiri. *The Fifty Years War: Israel and the Arabs*. London: BBC Books and Penguin, 1998.

Brookes, Peter. *A Devil's Triangle*. Lanham, MD: Rowman and Littlefield, 2005.

Brotton, Jeremy. *The Renaissance Bazaar: From the Silk Road to Michelangelo*. Oxford: Oxford University Press, 2002.

Burke, Jason. *Al Qaeda: Casting a Shadow of Terror*. London: I.B. Tauris, 2003.

Busch, Briton Cooper. *Britain, India and the Arabs, 1914–1921.* Berkeley and Los Angeles: University of California Press, 1971.

Cardini, Franco. *Europe and Islam.* Oxford: Blackwell, 2001.

Carson, D. A. (ed.) et al. *The New Bible Commentary: 21st Century Edition.* Downers Grove, IL: InterVarsity Press, 1994.

Catherwood, Christopher. *Why the Nations Rage: Killing in the Name of God* Lanham, MD: Rowman and Littlefield, 2002.

———. *Christians, Muslims and Islamic Rage.* Grand Rapids, MI: Zondervan, 2003.

———. *Winston's Folly.* London: Constable & Robinson, 2004.

Christensen, Eric. *The Northern Crusades.* Minneapolis: University of Minnesota Press, 1980.

Commins, David. *The Wahhabi Mission and Saudi Arabia.* London: I.B. Tauris, 2006.

Cook, David. *Understanding Jihad.* Berkeley: University of California Press, 2005.

Cook, M. A. *Muhammad.* Past Masters. Oxford: Oxford University Press, 1996.

———. *Koran: A Very Short Introduction.* Oxford: Oxford University Press, 2000.

Cooper, Barry. *New Political Religion.* Columbus, MO: University of Missouri Press, 2004.

Corbin, Jane. *The Base: In Search of Al Qaeda.* London: Simon and Schuster, 2002.

Crone, Patricia, and Cook, M. A. *Hagarism: The Making of the Islamic World.* London: Macmillan, 1997.

Delong-Bas, Natana. *Wahhabi Islam.* Oxford: Oxford University Press, 2004.

Esack, Farid. *The Qur'an: A User's Guide.* Oxford: Oneworld Publications, 2005.

Esposito, John. *Unholy War: Terror in the Name of Islam.* Oxford: Oxford University Press, 2002.

———. *Islam: The Straight Path* (3rd ed.). Oxford: Oxford University Press, 1998.

————. *The Islamic Threat: Myth or Reality?* (2nd ed.). Oxford: Oxford University Press, 1995.

————. *What Everyone Needs to Know About Islam.* Oxford: Oxford University Press, 2002.

————. (ed.). *The Oxford History of Islam.* Oxford: Oxford University Press, 1999.

Feldman, Noah. *After Jihad.* New York: Farrar Straus and Giroux, 2003.

Fellure, Jacob *The Everything Middle East Book.* Avon, MA: Adams Media, 2004.

Firestone, Reuven. *Jihad: The Origin of Holy War in Islam.* Oxford and New York: Oxford University Press, 1999.

Fitzsimmons, M. A. *Empire by Treaty: Britain and the Middle East in the Twentieth Century.* London: Ernest Benn, 1965.

Fletcher, Richard. *The Cross and the Crescent: Christianity and Islam from Muhammad to the Reformation.* London: Allen Lane, 2003.

France, John. *The Crusades and the Expansion of Catholic Christendom, 1000–1714.* London: Routledge, 2005.

Fregosi, Paul. *Jihad.* Amherst, NY: Prometheus Books, 1998.

Friedman, Thomas. *From Beirut to Jerusalem* (rev. ed.). New York: Anchor Books, 1995.

Fromkin, David. *A Peace to End All Peace.* New York: Henry Holt, 1989.

Gabrieli, Francesco. *Arab Historians of the Crusades.* Berkeley: University of California Press, 1969

Geisler, Norman. *When Critics Ask.* Grand Rapids, MI: Baker Book House, 1992.

Gerges, Fawaz. *The Far Enemy.* Cambridge, UK: Cambridge University Press, 2005.

Goldschmidt, Arthur. *A Concise History of the Middle East* (5th ed.). Boulder, CO: Westview Press, 1996.

Goody, Jack. *Islam in Europe.* Cambridge, UK: Polity Press, 2004.

Gorenberg, Gershom. *The End of Days: Fundamentalism and the Struggle for the Temple Mount* (2nd ed.). New York: Oxford University Press 2002.

Gunaratna, Rohan. *Inside Al Qaeda.* London: C. Hurst, 2002.

Hamilton, Jill. *God, Guns and Israel* Stroud, UK: Sutton, 2004.

Hillenbrand, Carole. *The Crusades: Islamic Perspectives.* Chicago: Fitzroy Dearborn, 1999.

Hodgson, Marshall. *Venture of Islam* (3 vols.: *The Classic Age of Islam, The Gunpowder Empires, The Expansion of Islam*). Chicago: University of Chicago Press, 1974.

Hoge, James, and Gideon Rose (eds.). *How Did This Happen: Terrorism and the New War.* New York: Public Affairs, 2001.

Holt, Mack. *The French Wars of Religion, 1562–1629.* Cambridge, UK: Cambridge University Press, 1995.

Holt, P. M., Bernard Lewis, and A. Lambton (eds.). *The Cambridge History of Islam* (2-vol. ed.). Cambridge, UK: Cambridge University Press, 1970.

Hourani, Albert. *A History of the Arab Peoples.* Cambridge, MA: Belknap Press, 1991.

———. *Emergence of the Modern Middle East.* London: Macmillan, 1981.

Ignatieff, Michael. *The Lesser Evil.* Princeton, NJ: Princeton University Press, 2004.

Janowski, James. *Egypt: A Short History.* Oxford: Oneworld Publications, 2000.

Jansen, Johannes J. G. *The Neglected Duty.* New York: Macmillan, 1986.

Johnson, James Turner. *The Holy War Idea in Western and Islamic Traditions.* University Park PA: Penn State University Press, 1997.

Juergensmeyer, Mark. *Terror in the Name of God.* Berkeley and Los Angeles: University of California Press, 2000.

Karsh, Ephraim, and Inari Karsh. *Empires of the Sand.* Cambridge, MA: Harvard University Press, 1999.

Keay, John. *Sowing the Wind: The Seeds of Conflict in the Middle East.* London: John Murray, 2003.

Kedourie, Elie. *The Chatham House Version.* London: Weidenfeld and Nicolson, 1970.

Kennedy, Hugh. *The Court of the Caliphs*. London: Weidenfeld and Nicolson, 2005.

———. *The Early Abbasid Caliphate*. London: Croom Helm, 1981.

———. *The Prophet and the Age of the Caliphates*. Harlow, UK: Longman, 1986.

Kepel, Gilles. *Jihad: The Trail of Political Islam*. Cambridge, MA: Belknap Press, 2002.

———. *The War for Muslim Minds: Islam and the West*. Cambridge, MA: Belknap Press, 2004.

———. *The Revenge of God*. Cambridge, UK: Polity Press, 1994.

Klieman, Aaron. *Foundations of British Policy in the Middle East*. Baltimore: Johns Hopkins University Press, 1970

Laiou, Angeliki, and Mottadeh Roy (eds.). *The Crusades from the Perspective of Byzantium and the Muslim World*. Washington, DC: Dumbarton Oaks, 2001.

Laquer, Walter (ed.). *Voices of Terror*. New York: Reed Press, 2004.

Larsson, J. P. *Understanding Religious Violence*. Aldershot, UK: Ashgate, 2004.

Lewis, Bernard. *Islam and the West*. Oxford: Oxford University Press, 1993.

———. *The Multiple Identities of the Middle East*. London: Phoenix, 1999.

———. *The Crisis of Islam: Holy War and Unholy Terror*. London: Weidenfeld and Nicolson, 2003.

———. *Islam in History*. Chicago: Open Court Press, 1993.

———. *What Went Wrong? Western Impact and Middle Eastern Response*. Oxford: Oxford University Press, 2002.

———. *The Muslim Discovery of Europe*. New York: W.W. Norton, 1982.

———. *The Assassins: A Radical Sect in Islam*. London: Phoenix, 2003.

———. *Cultures in Conflict: Christians, Muslims and Jews in the Age of Discovery*. New York: Oxford University Press, 1995.

———. *The Future of the Middle East*. London: Weidenfeld and Nicolson, 1997.

————. *From Babel to Dragomans: Interpreting the Middle East.* London: Weidenfeld and Nicolson, 2004.

————. *The Arabs in History* (6th ed.). Oxford: Oxford University Press, 1993.

————. *The Middle East.* London: Weidenfeld and Nicolson, 1995.

————. (trans.). *Islam: Volume 1: Politics and War.* New York, Oxford University Press, 1987.

Lippman, Thomas. *Understanding Islam.* (2nd rev. ed.). New York: Meridian, 1995.

Maalouf, Amin. *The Crusades Through Arab Eyes*, trans. Jon Rothschild. New York: Shocken Books, 1985.

McCarthy, Justin. *The Ottoman Peoples and the End of Empire.* London: Arnold, 2001.

Mack, Rosamond. *Bazaar to Piazza: Islamic Trade and Islamic Art, 1300–1600.* Berkeley and Los Angeles: University of California Press, 2002.

Macmillan, Margaret. *Peacemakers.* London: John Murray, 2001.

Madden, Thomas E. (ed.). *Crusades: The Illustrated History.* Ann Arbor: University of Michigan Press, 2004.

Manji, Irshad. *The Trouble with Islam.* Edinburgh: Mainstream Publishing, 2004.

Mansfield, Peter, and Nicholas Pelham. *A History of the Middle East.* Harmondsworth, UK: Penguin, 2003.

Napoleoni, Loretta. *Modern Jihad.* London: Pluto Press, 2003.

Nicholson, Helen. *The Crusades.* Westport, CT: Greenhill Press, 2004.

————. (ed.). *Palgrave Advances in the Crusades* Houndmills, Basingstoke, UK: Palgrave, 2005.

Noorani, A. G. *Islam and Jihad.* London: Zed Books, 2002.

O'Donovan, Oliver. *The Just War Revisited.* Cambridge: Cambridge University Press, 2003.

Ovendale, Ritchie. *The Longman Companion to the Middle East Since 1914* (2nd ed.). London: Longman, 1998.

Palmer, Alan. *The Decline and Fall of the Ottoman Empire.* New York: Barnes and Noble Books, 1994.

Pape, Robert. *Dying to Win: The Strategic Logic of Suicide Terrorism.* New York: Random House, 2005.

Partner, Peter. *God of Battles: Holy Wars of Christianity and Islam.* Princeton, NJ: Princeton, Uttar Pradesh, 1997.

Peters, Rudolph. *Jihad in Classical and Modern Islam.* Princeton, NJ: Markus Wiener, 1996.

Rashid, Ahmed. *Taliban.* New Haven, CT: Yale University Press, 2000.

———. *Jihad: The Rise of Militant Islam in Central Asia.* New Haven, CT: Yale University Press, 2002.

Riddell, Peter, and Peter Cotterell. *Islam in Context.* Grand Rapids, MI: Baker Book House, 2003.

———. *Islam in Conflict: Past, Present, Future.* Leicester, UK: InterVarsity Press, 2003.

Riley-Smith, Jonathan. *The Crusades: A Short History.* New Haven, CT: Yale University Press, 1987.

Robinson, Francis (ed.). *The Cambridge Illustrated History of the Islamic World.* Cambridge, UK: Cambridge University Press, 1996.

Ruthven, Malise. *A Fury for God: The Islamist Attack on America.* London: Granta, 2002.

———. *Islam in the World* (2nd ed.). Oxford: Oxford University Press, 2000.

———. *Fundamentalism: The Search for Meaning.* Oxford: Oxford University Press, 2004.

Saad-Ghorayeb, Amal. *Hizbu'llah: Politics and Religion.* London: Pluto Press, 2002.

Sachar, Howard. *The Emergence of the Middle East, 1914–1924.* New York: Knopf, 1969

Saikal, Amin. *Islam and the West.* Basingstoke, UK: Palgrave, 2003.

Sawar, Muhammad, and Brandon Toporov. *The Complete Idiot's Guide to the Koran.* New York: Pearson Education, 2003.

Schulze, Reinhard. *A Modern History of the Islamic World.* London: I.B. Tauris, 2000.

Shadid, Anthony. *The Legacy of the Prophet*. Boulder, CO: Westview Press, 2001.

Sheinbaum, Kim Ezra, and Jamal Hasan (eds.). *Beyond Jihad: Critical Voices from the Inside*. Bethesda, MD: Academica, 2006.

Sicker, Martin. *The Pre-Islamic Middle East*. Westport, CT: Praeger, 2000.

———. *The Islamic World in Ascendancy*. Westport, CT: Praeger, 2000.

———. *The Islamic World in Decline*. Westport, CT: Praeger, 2001.

———. *The Middle East in the Twentieth Century*. Westport CT: Greenwood, 2001.

Simons, Geoff. *Iraq: From Sumer to Post-Saddam*. Basingstoke, UK: Palgrave, 2004.

Smith, Riley. *What Were the Crusades?* Totowa, NJ: Rowman and Littlefield, 1977.

Spencer, Robert. *Islam Unveiled*. San Francisco: Encounter Books, 2002.

———. *The Politically Incorrect Guide to Islam (and the Crusades)* Washington, DC: Regnery, 2005.

Stern, Jessica. *Terror in the Name of God: Why Religious Militants Kill*. New York: Ecco, 2003.

Sumption, Jonathan. *The Albigensian Crusade*. London: Faber and Faber, 1978.

Taymiyya, Ibn. *The Goodly Word*, trans. and abridged, Ezzedin Ibrahim and Denys Johnson-Davies. Cambridge: Islamic Texts Society, 2003.

Tibi, Bassam. *The Challenge of Fundamentalism: Political Islam and the New World Disorder*. Berkeley and Los Angeles: University of California Press, 1998.

———. *Islam Between Culture and Politics*. Basingstoke, UK: Palgrave, 2001.

Trifkovic, Serge. *The Sword of the Prophet*. Salisbury, MA: Regina Orthodox Press, 2002.

Tripp, Charles. *A History of Iraq*. Cambridge, UK: Cambridge University Press, 2000.

Tyerman, Christopher. *Fighting for Christendom: Holy War and the Crusades*. Oxford: Oxford University Press, 2004.

————. *The Invention of the Crusades* (Toronto and Buffalo: University of Toronto Press, 1998).

Viorst, Milton. *In the Shadow of the Prophet: The Struggle for the Soul of Islam*. Boulder, CO: Westview Press, 2001.

Waines, David. *An Introduction to Islam*. Cambridge: Cambridge University Press, 1995.

Warraq, Ibn (ed.). *The Quest for the Historical Muhammad*. Amherst, NY: Prometheus Books, 2000.

————. *What the Koran Really Says*: Amherst, NY: Prometheus Books, 2002.

Watterson, Barbara. *The Egyptians*. Oxford: Blackwell, 1997.

Wells, Colin. *The Complete Idiot's Guide to Understanding Saudi Arabia*. New York: Pearson Education, 2003.

Wheatcroft, Andrew. *Infidels: The Conflict Between Christendom and Islam, 638–2002*. London: Viking, 2003.

Wiktorowicz, Quintan. *Radical Islam Rising*. Lanham, MD: Rowman and Littlefield, 2005.

Wood, John A. *Perspectives on War in the Bible*. Macon, GA: Mercer University Press, 1998.

Yapp, Malcolm. *The Making of the Modern Middle East, 1792–1923*. Harlow, UK: Longman, 1998.

Ye'or, Bat. *The Decline of Eastern Christianity Under Islam: From Jihad to Dhimmitude*. Cranbury, NJ: Associated University Presses, 1996.

————. *Islam and Dhimmitude: Where Civilizations Collide*. Cranbury, NJ: Associated University Presses, 2002.

Zadeh, Firooz. *Islam Versus Terrorism*. Twin Lakes, CO: Twin Lakes, 2003.

Index